Taking Up Space

Pavement Books
London, UK
www.pavementbooks.com

British Library Cataloguing in Publication Data.
A catalogue record for this book is available from the British Library.

ISBN: 978-0-9571470-6-5

Taking Up Space

edited by
Jamal Aridi and Jessica Glendennan

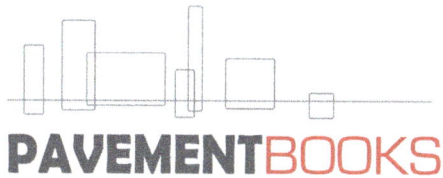

PAVEMENTBOOKS

STRANDS book series

A strand is a thread, a trajectory, a train of argument or thought. It is also a road, a promenade, the place where beach meets cityscape. It is a limit as well as a line. It is the site of encounter, conflict and confrontation. As borders are reinforced and sea levels rise, spaces of inclusion become those of exclusion. The strand gives way to the stranded, marooned, isolated, imprisoned and alienated. This series presents a range of perspectives and critical methodologies aimed at questions of space and our sociocultural engagement with it. As such it incorporates studies and approaches from cultural studies, literature, film and media studies, anthropology, political science, architecture and human geography.

Current and forthcoming titles

Return to the Street edited by Sophie Fuggle and Tom Henri

Taking Up Space edited by Jamal Aridi and Jessica Glendennan

La Ligne d'écume: Encountering the French Beach edited by Sophie Fuggle and Nicholas Gledhill

CONTENTS

ACKNOWLEDGMENTS

The support of the Goldsmiths Annual Fund that made publishing this book possible is gratefully acknowledged. We would like to thank student colleagues and staff in the Centre for Cultural Studies at Goldsmiths for the ecology they sustained: Paulius Yamin for his invaluable role as co-organizer of the Taking Up Space event; John Hutnyk, Nick Gledhill and Simon Barber who have contributed to the shaping of the conference; and Yaprak Aydin for her constant encouragement as co-organizer of the conference and for constructively proofreading the contributions. Gratitude must be given to Sophie Fuggle for devoting her time to making this publication happen, her editorial guidance and patience.

Special thanks to Manuel Ramos, Dina Khouri, Milia Ayache and Lynsey Meisner for their love and friendship.

NOTES ON CONTRIBUTORS

Maxwell Anley is in the process of completing a thesis with the title *The Wisdom of Brainless Knights: Paradox, Dialectics and Literature's Conditions of Possibility*. His research explores the paradoxical convergences between the thought of the Russian Formalists with that of Kant and Hegel.

Argos Aotearoa is a shoaling collective that has, at different times with different members, taken the form of a journal, an exhibition and a bus tour teach-in. In this iteration it involved Miri Davidson, who is a PhD student in London, and Stephen Turner, Anna Boswell and Sean Sturm, who teach at the University of Auckland and talk and write about settler histories and universities in geotheoretical terms.

Jamal Aridi received his MA from the Centre for Cultural Studies at Goldsmiths, University of London and currently lives in Beirut.

Edwina Attlee is a writer and researcher who recently completed a PhD with The London Consortium. *Strayed Homes: A Reading of Everyday Space* took as its topic the experience and representation of the launderette, the sleeper train, the fire escape, the greasy spoon and the postcard. You can find out about what she's up to now at http://cargocollective.com/sittingroom.

Christian Berkes is an urban planner. He works as a researcher and coordinator of projects addressing architectures, cities, technologies, and fictions. He co-developed, co-organized, and co-curated the international exhibition *Post-Oil City* (Germany, Japan, India, Croatia et al.) and the open discussion platform and blog 'The City and the Political' in Berlin. He is founder of the independent publishing house *botopress*.

Kenton Card is an urban analyst and practitioner. He co-launched a yearlong public knowledge project in Berlin: The City and the Political. His writings have been published in *Architectural Theory Review*, *Design Philosophy Papers*, *Horizonte: Zeitschrift für Architekturdiskurs*. Kenton's documentary films include 'Architecture for the Underserved,' 'Politics and the Political,' and 'Berlin's Urban Fights.' He has taught at Marlboro College, spoken at UC Berkeley, and been invited to lecture in New York City, London, Berlin, Beirut and Darmstadt. Kenton currently researches anti-displacement policies throughout California for lobbying state officials, and co-coordinates the CA statewide Residents United Network.

William Davis is a British-born designer and cultural analyst based in Malmö, Sweden. Working with research design and built environment: strategy, dialogue, analysis and experimentation, he has a background as an educator, facilitator, graphic design and scenography. William's project experience includes amongst others Brazil (SESC São Paulo, Studio-X Rio de Janeiro), Switzerland (ETH Zürich, BHSF, Camenzind), Germany (Chezweitz & Partners, Basics09, The Public School), Sweden (Malmö City Municipality, Malmö University, Media Evolution), Denmark (Copenhagen Municipality), Tanzania (Goethe Institute, Pro Helvetia).

Sophie Fuggle is lecturer in French at Nottingham Trent University. She is author of *Foucault/Paul: Subjects of Power* (Palgrave, 2013) and co-editor of *Word on the Street* (IGRS Books, 2011) and *Return to the Street* (Pavement Books, 2015). She is currently working on a collection focusing on the beach in the French cultural imagination. Her recent research looks at the framing of criminality within and beyond the French carceral space.

Karen García is a professional performance artist with several years experience as theatre actress, director, make-up artist and teacher. She is the founder and Artistic Director of 'La Loca de la Casa', a theatre company based in Bogotá, Colombia.

Jessica Glendennan is soon to be a storyteller at a library in Shanghai.

Marijn Nieuwenhuis is a lecturer in Political Geography in the Department of Politics and International Studies at the University of Warwick. His current research interests focus on the politics of the air which deals with questions of technology, pollution, security and the governance of the air. He can be contacted at : m.nieuwenhuis@warwick.ac.uk.

Catherine Taylor has an MA in Cultural Studies from Goldsmiths, University of London. She organised a tour of New Cross as part of the 'Taking up Space' Conference

Paulius Yamin is an anthropologist from the Universidad de los Andes (Bogotá, Colombia) with an MA in Cultural Studies from Goldsmiths, University of London. He works as an independent consultant in citizenship culture, cultural change and public policy for public and private organisations in Colombia and as a lecturer in anthropology.

INTRODUCTION

Jamal Aridi & Jessica Glendennan

Inevitably one has to be somewhere. The dimensions and rhythms that shape our surrounding render spaces multiple with no one single framework as a tool for analysis. Lefebvre tells us that knowledge emerges from spatially implemented practices, a landscape already there that allows a new representation of space to be formed. For example, perspective in Renaissance painting could only have developed as the architectural landscape in Italy underwent lavish growth (Lefebvre, 1992). Economic factors enabled such a transformation as forces of production and wealth increased. As money driven urban configurations transform cities like London or Beirut today, comparable here only in terms of endlessly ongoing construction, how are shifts in the landscape producing, erasing and reproducing representations? And what frameworks are employed to study cities as open systems? As for spaces that have not yet been made, how do they announce themselves?

Knowledge can also be considered movement through, into and out of the spaces we find ourselves in. Certainly relations to the spaces that surround us maintain our living between self-absorbed, isolated individuals and permeable beings open to encounter. The phrase *taking up space* itself holds opposite connotations as a call for responsibility toward surrounding and dwelling as well as a pejorative term ascribed to an unwelcome presence, and hints at a state of dispossession or exhaustion in a zone of alienation.

So far as physical space goes we begin from the body. The fictional landscape of cyberspace in William Gibson's genre defining novel *Neuromancer,* published in 1984, resonates today as a dimension of 'reality'. Part collective hallucination and part mirror, experienced by many people at the same time. Today's cyberspace forms networks reflective of Gibson's imagined description by similar metaphors freeing us from a physical 'already there' and to use this instant as the other side of a paradigm, knowledge takes place without being in a real space and does not presuppose the existence of physical space.

Virtual space dulls the body's presence - going there therefore not fully here. It functions as a mirror: my presence in a virtual reflected image on a surface/ screen that renders a virtual depth of field, and at the same time absence from the current position of my body (Foucault, 1984). Most often I find myself(s) in multiple positions at once.

The proliferation of spaces and presence in them maintain that we continue to ask questions on how to study these places whether 'real' or immaterial, on how general methodologies from (largely Western) philosophy and theory can be explicated in order to give knowledge that can be applied in different contexts, and on where one positions oneself critically while acknowledging the often subconscious nuances of complacency.

Spaces also function as the medium of the movement of temporality. The implications of circulated and reproduced time are inescapably as significant to consider as those of spaces in order to uphold critical approaches to spatio-temporal relations. Rather than privileging one over the other, capacities are hardly separable when it comes to intervention and analysis. Time flows and suspends in different rhythms and circulates, like the marketplace, in a system of relations given that labour and consumption function within a temporality subsumed, if not harnessed, for the maximization of human functionality.

In the process of compiling this collection one of the questions we asked ourselves was how is it relevant to publish these texts considering they were originally presented in a specific context? Calling our MA event at the Centre for Cultural Studies at Goldsmiths a conference might not offer a revealing description. The title *Taking Up Space* was our starting point to probe questions and forms of space in various manifestations. Investigating the space of the conference, however temporary, was a task to be carried out by all participants.

The contributions to this publication take on aspects and dimensions of space from different perspectives engaging with each other via meeting as well as diverging points. In Marijn Nieuwenhuis's 'Take a Breath' the variations of space and air interacting with each other are opened in immediate sense and surrounding before concepts. One way of beginning to think space lies in metaphor and abstraction but to begin from the body one must first get down and remember to breathe an air unfiltered. Alternatives to conceptions of space as either delineated or fluid meet practical exercises in Paulius Yamin and Karen García's 'Performing Spaces', who offer navigations to sensing space, such as performing balancing acts and playful engagements based on actor exercises from the Bogotá based *Colectivo La Loca de la Casa*. Bodily relations in contextual spaces uncover possibilities of movement within them as well as the traversal of various barriers.

Edwina Attlee's enthusiasm for tracing the edges of the urban facilitates 'Fire Escape', an examination of the connotations of fire escapes as interstices positioned for future use and at the same time barred from actualization. Rarely trodden paths such as fire drills invoke associations and actions of rehearsed chaos. 'City political workshop: discussing the political in space', led by Christian Berkes, Kenton Card and William Davis, aimed to explore interstices of the conference's meeting space. The anti-form workshop was partly transcribed and the printed transcripts present a discussion on the meaning of a political act as a positive engagement within a negative space.

Maxwell Anley's 'Sentimental Destruction' addresses the production of space and its ruination in Western accounts of Soviet culture. Tracing trajectories of power and ideology in 'dissident' Soviet novels within the soviet cultural field, his contribution challenges not only reductive monolithic notions but also those of dissent itself.

'Inland Drift: A Photo Essay' forms a latent interlude. A movement of images and text between seemingly non-contiguous places produces a retrograde account of time unrecountable and unaccounted for.

In their contribution titled 'Antipodean Topologies' Argos Aotearoa examines the fractured relations between past and present in the changing topos of Auckland. By excavating the University of Auckland's site operations, tensions of knowledge, commons and settler colonialism are unearthed. If the corporate university reproduces its conditions through a 'fractal' logic design as institutional model of a larger societal scale, then future alternatives cannot but consider brokenness and its implications for living well.

Throughout 'Visiting Hours' Sophie Fuggle delivers an informed discussion on the inseparability of work time and leisure time in contained amusement zones where economic, libidinal and temporal surplus are invested. Drawing on a visit to Attica prison in upstate New York and a critical reading of narratives of incarceration, prisons are framed as museified spaces where power still follows a disciplinary logic rather than more diffuse forms of power identified with contemporary capitalism to produce docile, industrious bodies.

Considering the contents of this publication in some way or another took place in New Cross, London, Catherine Taylor's tour map of SE14 is included and we invite you to use it as a template for your own walks.

References

Foucault, M. 1984. 'Des Espaces Autres'. *Architecture, Mouvement, Continuité* 5. October. 46-49.
Gibson, W. 1984. *Neuromancer*. New York, NY. Ace.
Lefebvre, H. 1992. *The Production of Space*. Trans. Donald-Nicholson Smith. Oxford. Blackwell.

TAKE A BREATH:
THE RELATIONSHIP BETWEEN AIR AND SPACE

Marijn Nieuwenhuis

Strepsiades: Socrates! my little Socrates!
Socrates [*loftily*]: Mortal, what do you want with me?
Strepsiades: First, what are you doing up there? Tell me, I beseech you.
Socrates [*pompously*]: I am traversing the air and contemplating the sun
(Aristophanes, *The Clouds*, 423 BC)

Take up the Air

This chapter attempts as much to uncover as to provide a meaning to the title of the workshop from which the collected chapters in this volume derive. The question of what it means to 'take up space' is thereby taken quite literally. When engaging with space we often fall back into metaphorical or conceptual abstractions of space. We talk of territory, of land, terrain, the global, the local etc. Rarely do we actually think about the question of what space actually is, how we are in space or how we are taken up by it. This chapter looks at the space that filters our bodies, the space which absorbs us, takes us up and which we take in. The space which we, in our obsession with the physical things *in*, *on* and *of* the earth, tend to forget, ignore or even consider unimportant. I take up the space of the air as a realm of inquiry, a possibility of imagination and as a body of knowledge, allowing a different way of sensing.

Take in the Air

The verb 'to take' refers to a whole range of activities. It is one of the primary and elementary words in perhaps any language. The Germanic original of its English variation derives, according to the *Oxford English Dictionary*, from the Gothic *têkan* which refers to a process of sensing with the hand. The use of the hand must be understood as the physical translation that makes possible the interaction between the subject and the exterior object. 'To take' relates to a process of transferal in which one is either on the end which seizes or appropriates; 'I take the blue pen', or on the end which accepts, 'I take this blue pen as a gift'. Something material or immaterial is, in other words, transferred to oneself by one's own action or through volition. The activity of taking allows for the communication, without and before language, between us and the world. To take means therefore also to give meaning and to create. Taking is worlding.

Having established the principles of the first word of this short chapter, it is perhaps time to dedicate some space discussing the second one. Engaging with the word 'space' is notoriously complex. Its Latin etymological origins, *spatium*, refer to a distance or a stretch. Elden (2013: 56) reminds us, for instance, that Caesar in his *Commentarii de Bello Gallico* (c. 58–49 BC) refers to spatium 'as distance or extent rather than space in the sense of a container'. The meaning of space for the ancient Greeks possessed instead metaphysical qualities. Space functioned more, but not exactly, like a receptacle. Casey (2009: 352) writes how Plato granted space (*chora*) a special elemental role in his cosmogony. It provided the necessary room ('space to be occupied') for existence, yet it was without design of itself in its original state. Chora was not a determined container, something that contains, neither was it determinable. It was its very non-determinedness which allowed for its distinctive receptiveness (Klein, 1989). Indeed, Derrida (1997: 10) notes that '[c]hora is the spacing that is the condition for everything to take place, for everything to be inscribed.' The Renaissance understanding of space, one which we still accept to be valid today, revolves instead around the idea of space as something both relative and calculable. What is interesting, at least for me here, is that the word and meaning of space refers to a historically heterogeneous and equally contingent number of things. The undetermined nature of space allows us to reopen debates on its meaning in the form of a question. What is space?

The third and final element of the title of this chapter refers to a particular act in which the two previously described words and concepts meet and interact. The act of breathing refers historically to an etiological and animating activity. The story of the creation of man (gender issues aside) starts in the *Bereishit*, or the 'Book of Genesis' (2:7), after all with God's breathing into the nostrils of Adam from which 'man became a living soul'. The 'father of Latin Christianity' Tertullian (2008: 186) writes in his treatise against Hermogenes' heretical doctrine of creation 'that the soul has its origin in the "breath" of God and did not come from matter'. Tertullian (ibid.: 202) notes in his critique that the soul and the breath are undividable and that the difference between them pertains to day and night. 'Why make a distinction between day and the light which pertains to day, when day is, really, only light?... Whenever question arises as to soul and breath, be sure that the soul *is* the breath just as day is the light [of day] itself. For, there is no difference between a being and that by which it is a being.'

The idea that breath instils souls is reflected in Paul's [3:16] famous last words to Timothy 'all Scripture is God-breathed [*pasa graphe theopneustos*]'. The word 'God-breathed' is rarely explicitly used in the Christian bible and derives from the equally uncommon Greek compound *theopneustos*. It etymologically refers to a combination of God (*theo*) and breath (*pneustos* from *pneo*). God's breathing-into the text translates into a divine form or process of 'inspiration' ['*inspirare*' or 'breathe-into']. The late Romanisation of the Greek word led to its translation of what we now commonly call 'divine inspiration'. Inspiration in its original, unsecular meaning embodies a spiritual exercise. The beautiful German word *Begeisterung* (literally: 'spiritualisation') and the older Greek word for inspiration, *enthousiasmos* (possessed by God or having God inside oneself), describe a process of possession and transformation by an external something. Hölderlin describes *Begeisterung* as the 'fundamental condition for the possibility of poetry' (Fenves, 2001: 127). The spirituality underlying the term continues to inform our secular understanding of the word. Shelley (1994: 81) writes in her *Defence of Poetry* that '[p]oets are the hierophants of an unapprehended inspiration.'

Inspiration can thus not be exclusively and calculatedly seized upon by the subject. The subject is, in the process of transferral, also the target of inspiration. The subject seizes but is also seized upon. The process is transformative insofar and in the sense that the subject takes a breath and is taken(-over) by breath. French feminist author Marguerite Duras in her contrasting account of male and female inspiration, writes that (female) inspiration is characterised by a process of being taken 'over'. 'The writing of women is really translated from the unknown, like a new way of communicating rather than an already formed language... I know that when I write there is something inside me that stops functioning... I let something take over inside me that probably flows from my femininity' (Duras, 1981: 174-5).

Take over the Air

I am not so much interested in either essentialising or distinguishing male from female forms of inspiration. This is not the place to do so. I rather want to discuss the something that flows inside and outside of the body, from me into you. The medium in which we, humans and other animals, function as filters, inhaling oxygen, exhaling carbon dioxide. It is the universal element which makes breathing possible and allows the subject to take and to be taken over by breath. This magical stuff is in more religious texts, as hinted at earlier already, the story of genesis. We moderns commonly describe it reductively (and thus problematically) simply as air. While breath allows for life, the air provides for breath. We do not really think about the air, it is taken for granted, invisible or, worse still, forgotten.

How different this was for the ancients whose world was so much larger than ours. Breath, air, mind and body were for pre-Socratic thinkers indistinguishably interconnected. The air is as the Greek monist thinker Anaximenes wrote 'beginning' (*arche*) and 'boundless' (*aperion*). In his discussion on Ionic philosophy Hegel (1995: 190) praises Anaximenes for pointing out 'what may be called the transition of natural philosophy into the philosophy of consciousness'. Old Greek theories of nature were however not separated from theories of mind or soul. The air was responsible for breathing soul into matter. 'As our soul, which is air, holds us together [*synkratei*], one spirit [*pneuma*] and air [*aer*] together likewise hold [*periexei*] the whole world [*kosmos*] together; spirit and air are synonymous' (Anaximenes quoted in ibid.). Infinite air is that 'which proceeds whatever comes to be or has done so in the past or will exist in the future, gods also and the divine. Everything else is made from its products [offspring or *genesis*]' (Anaximenes in Guthrie, 2000: 121).

Anaximenes also showed that through and because of air things change. When air is rarefied it becomes fire, when condensed it changes into wind, before it turns into a cloud, water, mud and earth and finally stones are shaped. The Anaximenean physical theory of change inspired Aristotle and Theophrastus to honour him with the title of 'the distant ancestor of the "objective" paradigm of scientific discourse' (Sandywell, 2003: 173). Yet, it was not Anaximenes who detached air from breath or soul from matter. Anaximenes rather aligned spirituality with nature or as Irigaray (1996: 123), in post-Anaximenean fashion, notes 'we transform our vital respiration into spiritual breath. Nature becomes spirit while remaining nature.'

It was instead Plato that planted the early seeds for the birth of the split between materiality and spirituality. Air became part of the four proportional and mathematically co-constituting elements [*stoicheia*] of the self-sustaining body of the earth [*soma*]. In Plato's *Timaeus* (2008) one can sense the emergence of a changing attitude towards the air. The air becomes democratically and proportionally aligned with the other elements to function as an almost materialistic building block for the great Demiurge, the divine craftsman or the 'God Geometer', who uses the elements to impose a strict regime of rational order onto and into the original natural chaotic and formless nature of space [*chora*]. Air is by Plato, in other words, classified as a product of necessity [*ananke*] and reason [*logos*], made serviceable to enforce order in *chora*. It is forcefully surrendered from its independent animating powers and becomes consequentially one among the other constituting elements. Air is after Plato also no longer attached to the soul, nor is it the manifestation of life. The elements are by Plato considered 'at best, dependent, quasi-entities, whose nominal and ontological status is insecure, fuzzy, fleeting' (Macauley, 2010: 153). It is gradually transformed as the instrument for the *becoming*, rather than the *being* itself of life.

While the air is gradually forgotten, the question of life, especially human life, becomes more important. Saint Paul's illustrious phrase *ta stoicheia tou kosmou* ('the elementary principles of the world') in his letter to the Galatians [4:9] still refers to the veneration of the elementary principles of the cosmos. Yet also here, the message conveyed is that the Galatians should forget the air and subordinate it along with the other elements to God's Law (Boer, 2007). Inspiration takes the form of transcendence. The air stops being the immanent force of life and is instead transformed into the medium through which God instils the soul. It is no longer the indistinguishable triangle of air, soul and breath which feeds the heart of our imagination. The lines between the three are instead separated by and subordinated to God. The final push that led to the severing of breath from spirit, matter from nature, ratio from myth, was, however, delivered by the moderns.

The 'discovery' of the instrumental function of the air remains a potent source for the scientific imagination. It provided knowledge about the historical possibility of plant photosynthesis and respiration while the unravelling of its secret composition granted the ingredients for the Industrial Revolution. Somewhere, however, between Plato and Joseph Priestley's discovery of oxygen, the air has lost its autonomy in the making of miracles and came to be submitted for dissection in the study of particles. It is no longer understood to do the essential giving that allows for the possibility of taking, in either the case of appropriation or volition. In the twenty-first century, we rather 'take' air as materially invisible, non-existent or disturbingly non-concrete. 'Things hang in the air'; 'things vanish into thin air'; 'things are up in the air'. Modernity is in fact defined by a compulsive need 'to clear the air' altogether.

Take Air

'To take air' refers not merely to a technical process of bodily seizing it. We do not breathe, smell or scent without being affected by the stuff that enters our bodies. The stuff of air is however not only the matter of oxygen, it is also the hidden source of what we now so blindly and ahistorically call 'inspiration'. We consume it without knowing; even our will is hopelessly equipped to refuse the air's alluring quality and sweet necessity. It precedes knowledge and slips past our cognitive gaze. It rather creates for the possibility of consciousness and challenges the *ratio* embedded in modern knowledge. Taking air is an unconscious and not a rational act. Maybe, therefore, it is not us at all who take air, but the air which takes us instead. It takes us historically, erotically, emotionally and imaginatively to distant memories, odours, situations and places. It does not merely move though space and time, it creates them.

However, it does much more even than 'inspire'. It provides, sustains and nurtures life; our life, animal life, plant life and, indeed, the lives of the Gods. Invisibly it creates *ex nihilio*; inscribing the world and designing it without the help of the Demiurge. Air, in other words, refers to something different than ontological, ontic and even theological being. It provides instead the very possibility of all three. It is *chora*, similarly without antecedent, reason or doubt. The air similarly as *Chora* 'provides a "situation" for things to come into existence and to take shape' (cf. Plato, 2008: 45; Plato in Macauley 2010: 158). One does not take air without being taken by it, possessed not by God, but by air itself. Air takes.

References

Boer, M. C. d. 2007. 'The Meaning of the Phrase τα στ[omicron]ιχεια τ[omicron]υ κ[omicron]σμ[omicron]υ in Galatians.' *New Testament Studies* 53.2. 204-224.

Casey, E. 2009. *Getting back into Place*. Bloomington, IN. Indiana University Press.

Derrida, J. and P. Eisenman.1997. 'Transcipt One'. *Chora L Works: Jacques Derrida and Peter Eisenman*. J. Kipnis and T. Leeser. New York, NY. The Monacelly Press.

Duras, M. 1981. 'From an Interview [1975]'. In E. Marks and I. de Courtivron (eds). *New French Feminisms*. Brighton. Harvester. 174-5.

Elden, S. 2013. *The Birth of Territory*. Chicago, IL. University of Chicago Press.

Fenves, P. D. 2001. *Arresting Language: From Leibniz to Benjamin*. Stanford, CA. Stanford University Press.

Guthrie, W. K. C. 2000. *A History of Greek Philosophy: Volume 1, The Earlier Presocratics and the Pythagoreans*. Cambridge. Cambridge University Press.

Hegel, G. W. F. 1995. *Lectures on the History of Philosophy: Greek Philosophy to Plato*. Lincoln, NE. University of Nebraska Press.

Irigaray, L. 1996. *I Love to You: Sketch for a Felicity Within History*. London. Routledge.

Klein, J. 1989. *A Commentary on Plato's Meno*. Chicago, IL. University of Chicago Press.

Macauley, D. 2010. *Elemental Philosophy: Earth, Air, Fire, and Water as Environmental Ideas*. New York, NY. State University of New York Press.

Plato. 2008. *Timaeus and Critias*. Oxford. Oxford University Press.

Sandywell, B. 2003. *Presocratic Reflexivity: The Construction of Philosophical Discourse c. 600-450 BC. Logological Investigations Volume 3*. London. Routledge.

Shelley, P. B. 1994. *A Defence of Poetry. The Defence of Poetry Fair Copies: A Facsimile of Bodleian MSS (E. 6 And. D. 8. Vol. 20).* M. O'Neill. London. Routledge.

Tertullian. 2008. *On the Soul. The Fathers of the Church; Tertullian, Apologetical Works and Minucius Felix, Octavius.* Tertullian. New York, NY. Catholic University of America. 165-312.

PERFORMING SPACES

Paulius Yamin & Karen García
Colectivo La Loca de la Casa, Bogotá, Colombia[1]

This text is aimed at introducing a series of exercises regularly used to train actors. Our focus will be those exercises which are meant to develop different ways of learning, experiencing, moving, feeling and discovering the spaces around us in order to be able to *perform* in them. That is, we want to introduce some basic practices which are useful in developping a certain sensibility towards space, towards its possibilities. So when in the title we speak about performing (spaces), we are certainly not only speaking of actors locked into a theatre: we are speaking of every*body*, of the possibilities that each one of us has and of the ways in which we can take up, occupy, cross, represent, write, research and perform space.

The theatre stage might seem like a contained space and yet, within its limits, it contains the whole world. Or at least a rehearsal of the whole world. In between its three (or four) walls, different places, imagined or remembered but made possible for a specific performance, are *enacted* together with the emotions, conflicts and passions of the characters portrayed. To look into the practice of theatre for insights on the subject of space and our relationship with it, isn't useful because 'the city is a theatre' or because 'we all behave like actors' in our everyday lives. Sentences like those are quite unfortunate, we believe, because the sense in which they are used carries with it something like an academic bad faith: they completely ignore the processes that make a performance possible and limit themselves to the perspective of a spectator who doesn't want to know anything about how the play was done, about the work or abilities necessary to perform it. Through such sentences theatre, and actors, are used as labels for something phony, as a technique of faking that we use when we meet others in order to attain certain ends. This is not what acting or performing a play involves or requires (which becomes clear by reviewing Stanislavsky's most basic ideas). Otherwise, that same spectator will end up watching not a play, not

---

[1] Independent theatre group based in Bogotá, Colombia. Founded in 2006 and directed from the beginning by Karen García, the group performs regularly in several theatres around the city and hosts regular workshops on acting, voice training and artistic makeup. For further information go to www.lalocadelacasa.com or write to info@ lalocadelacasa.com.

characters, but a group of actors trying hopelessly to look and act like someone who, we almost immediately, in each action and each word, get the irresistible impression they are not. But of course, how many times have we all seen plays where we have this very impression? Here a possible antidote might take the form of a sentence used by Karen García to open her acting courses: an actor never acts, he *is* in situation.

An example of this bad faith is Richard Sennett's book *The Fall of Public Man* (1978), which includes a chapter called 'Man as Actor' where he examines the 'public realm' of urban life in the 18th century. Here (following Diderot) acting in society, in the 'public realm', consists of the 'tricks of the stagecraft' through which artifice dominates the expression of emotions (Sennett, 1978: 111). This sense for the metaphor of the city as theatre not only ignores how characters and spaces are built and worked through for a theatrical performance, but it also closes its creative possibilities (because it implies that the text that people interpret and speak in their everyday life is somehow rehearsed, it remains in a certain order mediated by a technique of cold-heartedly telling lies). What this metaphor maintains, in the end, is the egotistical social being which only follows his own interests to the point of manipulating others.

Looking into the practice of theatre for insights on space is useful as a counterpoint to this because it introduces certain sensibilities, certain ways of discovering space with our bodies, our voices, our possibilities... Through those exercises, space is walked through in different directions, rhythms and 'modes of awareness', space is described in terms of our own position within it (the position of our bodies) and the feelings it inspires, space is made possible only by virtue of our relationship with other people, of what we are doing and what they are doing and how different or similar our gestures are, space is modified by taking it to be a 'tray' that must be balanced with the weight of our bodies and the positions we adopt within it.

The ideas and practices which make the work of actors on a stage possible (and indeed any space can be transformed into a stage) provide a useful alternative to thinking about space either as a container or as something that enables different flows (and by introducing those metaphors here, which are regularly used in sociological debates around space (Knowles, 2010), we are of course also engaging with the subject of the space of the city). That is, I cannot physically go through that wall, but I can turn this whole place into somewhere else with my words, with my disguises, with my gestures and my movements. In one way or another, the walls of the stage are transcended in each performance, either because we pretend we are somewhere else (the theatre is turned into a living room or a kitchen) because we make reference to other contexts (as when the actors express, from the space of the stage, their emotions and past experiences).

Figure 1. Karen García directing an exercise where actors are asked to mimic what the other is doing, while at the same time maintaining a certain balance in space (as if the space they are performing in was a tray that must be kept balanced with the weight of their bodies (photo taken by Paulius Yamin on 17/4/2012).

The theatre stage is a space that is always meant to mutate into some other context: a small house in Sweden, a castle in Denmark, a ranch in Colombia. And it also gives us the possibility of creating a ranch in Denmark and a castle in Colombia: the stage is where the theatre happens, or it is the theatre itself, but precisely because of this, it is also some place completely different (but without becoming that place completely either). The theatrical space, the performing space, is not defined by complete stillness or immediacy, but neither by complete movement or evocation: rather it works in the manner of a disguise which is meant to create a powerful evocation. This is because theatre introduces a narrative: commenting on Michel de Certeau, Michael Sheringham (2006) argues that the everyday narrative performances 'link different spaces together, like metaphors. Stories build bridges and in so doing transgress limits.' (Sheringham, 2006: 227). A narration, de Certeau points out, 'does not describe a practice, or contents itself with expressing a motion. It performs it' (quoted in Sheringham, 2006: 231). With those narrative performances, established orders and stable systems are subverted. Something is produced here: not some kind of account or description of space, but a way of using it and of then re-creating it (that is, a way of performing it). 'Reality and fiction are intertwined,' Augusto Boal (2001: 62) reminds us, 'but we know that fiction is always one of the multiple forms of reality, as real as any' (ibid). The space of the stage is always on the brink of being elsewhere and what defines it is not containment or fluidity, but rather the relationships of the characters that dwell in it.

But with all this in mind, how do we learn to perform in space? How do we discover and experience space in order to perform in it? There are of course many possible ways, but we want to suggest just a few examples of some quite basic exercises that actors often use, and that we believe researchers of space should start using more often. The exercises are not, by any means, new or even uncommon, but they are very helpful in illustrating how this sensibility towards space might work. Each introduces a teaching and a possibility.

Almost every one of our rehearsals or training sessions begins by walking through a certain space (the room we have rented for rehearsals or the stage in which we are going to perform). This walk must be done avoiding an established direction, avoiding circles or using the same paths over and over. Then, everybody stops and one person (we would like to avoid the word 'actor' here because in this particular discussion it could be replaced by any other word), is asked to describe how they *are* placed in space: each muscle that is supporting their body, how they feel in it, what features of it call their attention. Those practices aim to answer the question: *how am I in space?*

After this, it is useful to move through space in different ways, always trying to identify which muscles and body parts, and which sensory and emotional responses, are involved in each way of moving. This includes walking following a straight line and in circles, in zigzags, forwards or backwards... Any way the person doing it can think of. At certain moments, the director will tell them to stop and to pay attention to every feature of the space they are in (its smell, its colours, its sounds, its possible resemblances to other contexts, to the memories it brings in each one, etc.). This is meant to waken the senses and the emotions together with the body and with how we experience that particular space, while at the same time laying emphasis, from there, on our possibility of moving through that space (not a barrier we cannot cross or something we can dominate only by looking at it, but the possibility of traversing and acknowledging it with our own bodies).[2]

In another exercise, which is called 'the tray', a single leader is designated while the rest of the participants have to balance the space as if they were all standing on a tray. All of the other participants must mimic the movements of the leader, but always being on the opposite corner of the space in order to balance the tray without touching each other. With this exercise people are

---

[2] On this subject, while watching the city of New York from above, Michel de Certeau (2002: 92) asks himself: 'To what erotics of knowledge does the ecstasy of reading such a cosmos belong? Having taken a voluptuous pleasure in it, I wonder what is the source of "seeing the whole," of looking down on, totalizing the most immoderate of human texts'. He continues: 'The panorama-city is a "theoretical" (that is, visual) simulacrum, in short a picture, whose condition of possibility is an oblivion and a misunderstanding of practices. The voyeur-god created from this fiction, who, like Schreber's God, knows only cadavers, must disentangle himself from the murky intertwining behaviors and make himself alien to them' (Certeau, 2002: 93).

allowed to play with space through their relationship with other people. The point here is not whether we can 'really' balance space and play with it, or if we are ever going to encounter a situation where we will have to stand in a tray in 'real life' and balance it, but rather to awaken and rehearse certain sensibilities and possibilities of engaging with space (the ability of 'hearing' with our bodies, which allows us to communicate with others without speaking is indispensable to perform on a stage, for example). In addition to the actions that work as training, before each presentation the people that are to perform in a certain space must ideally take some time to recognize it: to walk through it, to feel it, to look for its possibilities and illuminations and to adjust the sounds of their bodies according to its shape, size, materials and reverberations.

The specific exercises we chose to report here allowed us to follow a path that went from the question '*how am I in space?*' to the action of experimenting with how we can move through space and perceive it, and then to an active engagement with that space that is only possible through our relationship with others. With those exercises, as with most exercises which follow in one way or another the Stanislavsky method (see 2008a and 2008b), the central objective is to get rid of, as far as is possible, our habitual gestures and ways of moving and engaging with space in order to open up our own possibilities. This is because we don't want all of our characters to walk, speak or move like us, or even feel or react in the same ways as we do ourselves. As Augusto Boal puts it, 'It is necessary for the actor to feel certain emotions and sensations that he had lost the habit of feeling, to expand his capacity to express himself and feel' (Boal, 2001: 106). From that moment on, you can start creating characters from your own habits or ways of moving and feeling or from those of other people you know or you have seen, but also from machines, animals, from the way you perceive fire, water, or wind (their movement, the emotions they engender in you). In short, you can create ways of moving, feeling and experiencing space (that is, characters) from emotions, ideas, experiences...

'In the oldest sense of the term,' Augusto Boal tells us,

> theatre is the capacity that human beings have (and which is absent in animals) of observing themselves in action. Humans are capable of seeing themselves in the act of seeing, capable of thinking their emotions and being moved by their thoughts. They can see themselves here and picture themselves over there, they can see themselves as they are now and picture themselves as they will be tomorrow (Boal, 2001: 26, emphasis added).

Theatre, then, can be a way of learning and language that is useful for finding new sensibilities, new ways of experiencing and performing. Following Boal's ideas (see Boal, 2008), 'dramatic action' should not replace 'real action,' but rather works as a rehearsal or a learning experience for it. Rather than a finished version of the world, this makes possible the *questions* which allow us to engage with different possibilities. It is up to us to formulate the answers, to propose the alternatives. Pointing out a particular lamp on the stage where they were rehearsing, Stanislavsky once said to his students:

> You know, it's not the object itself, the bulb, that causes us to concentrate, but an idea your imagination suggests. This idea gives it new life, and, aided by the given circumstances, makes the object interesting. Create a wonderful and interesting story round it. Then this detestable bulb will be transformed and become a stimulus to creative activity (Stanislavsky, 2008a: 110).

The sensibility reviewed here is meant to bring about different paths (new or old, we are not quite sure) for both research and intervention in the ways we study and experience space. That is why we don't want to make it too explicit. Those practices just stand as examples of how we can experience and recognize space (or specific spaces) in order to perform in it, whether we are occupying it, walking through it, researching or planning it. Through these, the space works as a creative *possibility* that is only attainable if we learn how to engage with it using our own bodies and sensibilities.

References

Boal, A. 2001. *Juegos para actores y no actores*. Barcelona. Alba Editorial.
_____ . 2008. *Theatre of the Oppressed*. London. Pluto Press.
de Certeau, M. 2002. *The Practice of Everyday Life*. Berkeley, CA. University of California Press.
Knowles, C. 2010. 'Mobile Sociology'. *The British Journal of Sociology* 61. 373 - 379.
Sennett, R. 1978. *The Fall of Public Man*. London. Vintage.
Sheringham, M. 2006. *Everyday Life: Theories and Practices from Surrealism to the Present*. Oxford. Oxford University Press.
Stanislavsky, K. 2008a. *An actor's work: a student's diary*. London. Routledge.
_____ . 2008b. *My life in art*. London. Routledge.

FIRE ESCAPE

Edwina Attlee

This essay is about the space of the fire escape and how it functions, or does not function, in the city. It will gesture towards where my research into these spaces might lead me and hopefully open up some discussion about its possibilities.

Writing about the urban planning taking place in Paris during the 1970s and 80s Michel de Certeau speaks about the presence of 'defaced houses and closed down factories' in the newly renovated and regenerated areas of the city. He describes these buildings as *obstacles* and *resistances*. Obstacles and resistances to the newly arranged space and newly ordered *time* of the city. He writes that 'by eluding the law of the present, these inanimate objects acquire a certain autonomy. . . they no longer have the contents which tame the strangeness of the past with meaning' (Certeau, 2002: 135-6). I would like to suggest that the fire escapes of London's buildings today operate in a similarly disruptive and resistant fashion. The closed down factories and derelict houses of Certeau's Paris work like dead metaphors in the text of the cityscape. They are familiar but empty, divorced from their original meaning. The way we look at, pass by, use and misuse the fire escape is akin to when we skip or gloss over an unfamiliar or *over*-familiar word or phrase in a text. Ignorant of the literal or historic truth behind these phrases or spaces we take in the symbol but not what it actually signifies, glancing over it quickly, forming enough of a picture from its edges. Fire escapes lend themselves to this treatment partly because they are all edges. They are both spatial and temporal places of an absence staged by a presence, an emptiness made significant, a future tense that is both pointed to and ignored by the present; a future tense made present.

This sense of them being like dead metaphors is born out even in their name. The words 'fire' and 'escape' are words of urgency, potency and disaster. But the coupling 'fire escape' is mundane, colourless and completely separate from the kind of active impetus that we might assume such a pairing would induce. The fire escape has been subsumed into that other, dead coupling of words, 'Health and Safety'. Nothing seems more certain to induce in an audience a soporific, somnolent acquiescence than this awful pairing. I have said that the structures enact a staging of absence. What I mean by this is that they are, by law and by necessity, empty spaces. Anyone who has worked in a theatre or school knows that the fire exit and escape must always be 'kept clear'. Steven Connor has written that buildings are 'articulations of air' (Connor, 2004), fire escapes seem to be articulations of pregnant air; they are somehow fuller in their emptiness. They are spaces which must allow for the passage of a large number of people in a limited amount of time and therefore they must be pathways, simple to use and direct. This *use* is problematic however, for the fire escape is built in the hope that it will never be used. In one sense we might call the fire escapes *wastes* of space, for they must be some of the most un-trodden routes in the city.

They form the spatial counterpart to that routine *waste* of time; the fire drill. The fire drill is a bizarre exercise, steeped as it is in the oddly mythic practice of pre-enactment,[1] a placating of the gods, a rehearsal for that which you hope will never happen. As a temporal exercise the drill is anomalous in our day-to-day experience for, here is reasonable time-tabled delay, sponsored or enforced delinquency. Connor has written that 'fire precaution requires an intensification of regulated movement – clearly marked exits, drills that reduce the random millings and effusiveness of social movements into controlled routines' (Connor, 2004). But in fact these drills never run smoothly, they are never experienced as regulated or controlled for they cannot lose their innate character which is chaotic. You are taken out of work and *allowed* (forced even) to stand idle, this is not something we find easy to do. The fire drill is meant to catch people unawares, and as such the milling crowd assembled at the 'assembly point' are always in a state of not-quite-readiness. They are without coats (due to the *insistence* that they pick up none of their belongings), they are bleary eyed. Whether they interrupt the school or work day the drill always seems to take longer than it should, and those participating are left with an overall feeling of both inefficiency and anti-climax. Which is not to say that people wish there had been a fire, but rather that the drill would seem more point-full if there had been.

Part of the reason the drills are so shoddily performed is that they work with the conceit of a fake now, a pretence, a play. People resist this, dawdling, stopping to pick up their things or finish what they are doing, they do not *believe* and therefore do not play along with the fictitious emergency. So it is partly that the spaces are made into spaces of make-believe by Health and Safety rituals that the fire escape has come to function like a dead metaphor or like a word that we do not fully understand. It is partly also because of the alternative uses or misuses of the spaces. Because fires are (thankfully) rare, the ways in which we use the structures are almost always forms of misuse or abuse. In film and literature the fire escape has been used to gain access to or exit from a building that you're probably not meant to be accessing or exiting. We can think of the structures in *Rear Window* (1954) or *Breakfast at Tiffany's* (1961) where characters use the

---

[1] A term suggested to me by Francessca Cavallo.

drop down ladders to escape to the street or to gain easy access to one another's bedrooms.

We can think of chase scenes with the mounting suspense of stairwell after stairwell, or the scurried detour as someone leaving a building desperately tries to avoid meeting someone coming up in a lift. Lovers and thieves are all advised to 'take the stairs' or 'use the fire escape.' It is both trap and short cut, escape route and hiding place. A moment of the characteristically subversive ingress allowed for by the fire escape takes place in Michael Chabon's *Amazing Adventures of Kavalier and Clay*:

> Joe let go of the ladder with his right hand, snatched a puff from his cigarette, then replaced it. Then he took hold of the ladder again and swung himself, throwing his entire body into it, with each swing describing an increasingly wider arc. The ladder rattled and chimed against the fire escape. Suddenly he folded himself in half, let go of the ladder completely, and allowed his momentum to jackknife him out, up and over, onto the bottom platform of the fire escape, where he landed on his feet. It was a completely gratuitous performance, done purely for effect or for the thrill of it; he could easily have pulled himself up the ladder hand over hand, he could easily have broken his neck (Chabon, 2000: 111-12).

Here we have a definite performance, linking back to the sense of the escape as a space of make believe or play. For the character Joe it is a fortuitous space of dramatic exposure –the escape allows for and even invites this kind of spectacle because of their elevated and exposed position but also because they are somehow outside of normal rules. Are escapes inside or outside the space of the home? Are they private or public? This sense of them being somehow ungovernable, or at least un-policed, means that they are also spaces of abuse; we can think of drug deals, illicit sexual encounters, and the fact that the escapes offer refuge to those who want to hide, or those who do not have a place of their own to be in. And this has always been a problem with fire escapes, if they can be used to get out, they can be used to get in.

As we have said, fire escapes are *all edges*, (whether old fashioned appendages to buildings or, the more familiar modern spaces of hollowed out internal stairwells); they surround empty space. They are both spatial and temporal places of an absence staged by a presence, an emptiness made significant. Barthes writes of tempura (delicately battered Japanese vegetables or fish) that they are 'clump[s] of emptiness' (Barthes, 2005: 24), caught as they are between batter and between chopsticks. This sense of an intensity of nothingness, a weighted congealed, compacted gap or space is what is so arresting for me about the space of fire escapes; the strange 'articulation of air' that they enact draws attention to absence through presence. Still writing about tempura Barthes marvels at the paradox of a 'purely interstitial object', this is an object made up purely of intervening spaces, the chinks of crevices between things. In Physics the interstice is the space between adjacent atoms or ions in a crystal lattice so we can get some sense of the minute and delicate fabric of spaces that Barthes is alluding to. In James Schuyler's 'An East Window on Elizabeth Street' the fire escape is 'sky-aspiring' and 'miraculous', both sensible and magical, peeling its way around simultaneously lived lives, calling attention to the structure of the building. The drama of space and structure, the drama of the interstice, creates a vibrant and voyeuristic panorama.

> I don't know how it can look so miraculous,
> An organic skin for the stacked cubes of air
> People need, things forcing up through the thick unwilling air
> Obstinate and mindless as the glorious swamp flower
> Skunk cabbage and the tight uncurling punchboard slips
> Of fern fronds. Toned, like patched, wash-faded rags.
> Noble and geometric, like Laurana's project for a square.
> Mutable, delicate, expendable, ugly, mysterious
> (seven stories of just bathroom windows)
> Packed: a man asleep, a woman slicing garlic thinly into oil
> (what a stink, what a wonderful smell)
> Burgeoning with stacks, pipes, ventilators, tensile antennae-
> That bristling gray bit is part of a bridge,
> That mesh hangar on a roof is to play games under.
> But why should a metal ladder climb, straight
> And sky-aspiring, five rungs above a stairway hood
> Up into nothing? (Schuyler, 1981: 58)

Barthes goes on to compare the tempura chef who fabricates his creations in front of an audience to the calligrapher who works at a similarly public stall or table. He calls the interstice 'an empty sign' and writes that the chef (like the calligrapher) 'accomplishes in the racket of the restaurant, a hierarchized arrangement, not of time but of *tenses*' (Barthes, 2005: 26). I think what he means by this distinction is that the calligrapher and the tempura chef hold various tenses still at once; they isolate and ossify instances which do not necessarily follow one another but which stand separate but side by side without disrupting one another to the point of destruction or nonsense. So the various incarnations of the tempura can be displayed simultaneously just as a sentence can negotiate various tenses at once. This paused ambiguity is also what is taking place in the language of fire precaution. If we take this pub sign as an example we notice an interesting combination of tenses, the glib sensibility of 'Unless, of course, there is a fire', points to a rather perverse acceptance of the possible disaster made somehow more emphatic through the double stretch of asterisk and parenthesis.

STRICTLY NO
EXIT / ENTRY
VIA
FIRE ESCAPE*

SMOKERS PLEASE GO THRU
MAIN PUB TO SMOKE
OUTSIDE

[*unless of course there's a fire.]

Figure 1. Sign in The Scolt Head, Stoke Newington, London. Photograph by the author. May 2012.

It is this disruption of time that means that the fire escapes, like the derelict buildings or closed down factories identified by Certeau, operate in some way as both obstacles and resistances. Certeau would place them and our appropriation of them in his 'network of anti-discipline' because they work against habit, routine and control.[2] Certeau suggests that it is in their dereliction, in their uselessness, in their appropriation of 'a nothing' that the buildings become gener-

---

[2] 'the clandestine forms taken by the dispersed, tactical and makeshift creativity of groups or individuals already caught in the nets of "discipline"' (Certeau, 2002: xiv-xx).

ative spaces: 'Not because of what they say or do but because their strangeness is silent, as well as their existence, concealed from actuality. Their withdrawal makes people speak –it generates narratives –and it allows action; through its ambiguity, it "authorizes" spaces of operation' (136).

I have said that the fire escapes operate like dead metaphors, we tend to ignore them if we see them; they do not mean what they once might have meant. My research will investigate the spaces and the way they are used. Can this use be aligned to the daydream? Certeau cites Guy Rololato's claim that 'I read and I daydream, my reading is thus a sort of impertinent absence'(173). Jean Baudrilliard writes, 'blessed, beneficent, is anything that takes us into the unwilled, into dreamlike disengagement from our own lives' (Baudrillard, 2008: 77) In the same text, about game playing and make believe, Baudrillard marries 'the tactile detour of streets' with 'the tactile detour of ideas' (81). I am interested in linking Certeau's sense of 'anti-discipline' with Solantro's sense of the 'impertinent absence' that takes place when someone reads and daydreams. Daydreaming is unbidden, unproductive and diachronic and the space of the fire escape, out of time, a waste of space, used almost exclusively for reasons other than its function. My research will ask what it means to use a space in this way, and whether the spaces can be said to effect the environment they are part of and the people in it.

It may seem fanciful or overly poetic to align, as Baudrillard does, 'the tactile detour of streets' with 'the tactile detour of ideas', and yet, our everyday experience as well as scientific research, shows us that this is in fact a literal rather than metaphorical truth (or the literality of the metaphorical). Space, memory, the city and the subconscious are intricately woven with one another. Research carried out by psychologists at the University of Notre Dame explores the relationship of certain spaces on memory. The researchers have put forward Event Boundary Theory which examines the everyday occurrence of forgetting what you went into a room for. The theory asserts that when you walk through a door your short-term memory registers it as an event and 'memory, for recently experienced information, is affected by the structure of the surrounding environment' (Radvansky et al, 2011) The experiments have shown that the action of walking through a door disturbs short-term memory and that the more doors you walk through, the more you forget. Starting from the event boundary of the doorway I want to think meaningfully about the relationship between space and memory with the structure of the fire escape as my tool. Certeau identifies resistance in the autonomous objects of Paris, the fire escape is structurally empty, temporally distorting, and ubiquitous. Can the spaces be read as eliciting a certain way of thinking and feeling? Can they be said to alter memory? Can they be said to alter the experience of the cityscape? They are spatially and temporally permeable – what is the effect of this permeability and how can it be measured?

References

Barthes, R. 2005. *Empire of Signs*. Translated by Richard Howard. New York, NY. Anchor Books.

Baudrillard, J. 2008. The Jean Baudrillard Reader. Edited by Steve Redhead. New York, NY. Columbia University Press.

de Certeau, M. 2002. *The Practice of Everyday Life*. Berkeley, CA. University of California Press.

Chabon, M. 2000. *The Amazing Adventures of Kavalier and Clay*. London. Harper Perennial.

Connor, S. 2004. 'Building Breathing Space': A lecture given at the Bartlett School of Architecture, 3rd March.

Radvansky, G.A. et al. 2011. 'Walking through doorways causes forgetting: further extrapolations'. *The Quarterly Journey of Experimental Psychology* 64.8: 1632-1645.

Schuyler, J. 1981. 'An East Window on Elizabeth Street' in *Collected Poems*. London. Carcanet.

NEW CROSS
A GUIDED TOUR

THIS IS THE MAP FOR A GUIDED TOUR UNDERTAKEN IN NEW CROSS, LONDON ON THE 25TH JUNE 2012.

THE MAP IS HAND IN THE MIDDLE — WITHOUT ADDITIONAL TEXTUAL PROMPTS) WAS GIVEN OUT TO PARTICIPANTS.

THE MAP AND ROUTE WERE DESIGNED TO BE FLEXIBLE TO ALLOW FOR NEW EXPERIENCE AND DISCUSSION AROUND THE STREET SPACE.

THE 5 BLACK CIRCLES ALLOW THE PARTICIPANT R TO BE GUIDED BY BASIC VISUAL INFORMATION AND

THE TOUR GUIDE PROVIDES INFORMATION ON THE PLACES OF INTEREST (WRITTEN ON THE RIGHT). THE MORE INFORMATION

THE PARTICIPATOR GETS, THE MORE RECOGNISABLE THE MAP BECOMES.

THE PROPOSED ROUTE MARKED ON THE MAP ALLOWS FOR A BASIC SENSE OF DIRECTION AND MOVEMENT AND THE MAP HAS FEW IDENTIFYING FEATURES TO ENABLE THE PARTICIPATOR TO ADD THEIR OWN VISUAL CUES CREATING AN EXPERIENCE OF NEW CROSS STREET SPACE THROUGH TIME, MEMORY AND MOVEMENT.

1 STARTING POINT
GOLDSMITHS UNIVERSITY
INTRODUCTION TO WALK
ACT OF WALKING : SPACE → MOVEMENT
MOVEMENT ← TIME

2 FORDHAM PARK
MOVEMENT AND EXPERIENCE
LAYOUT OF PARK — TOWN PLANNING — HOW DO WE EXPERIENCE THE PARK THROUGH MOVEMENT? FUNCTION OF PARK / OPEN SPACES. PATHWAYS FOR CONTROLLED EXPLORATION.
SCHOOL USE. LACK OF PRIVATE GARDENS + GREEN SPACE REDEVELOPMENT.

3 LAURIE GROVE
TRACE OF ROAD SIGN
LAYER OF TIME — SPACE AS HISTORY
SIGN AS FORM OF CODING, HIGHLY CODIFIED SYSTEM — LONDON ROAD SIGNS. DIRECTS US AND NAVIGATES US.
TRACE AS LAYER → SURFACE — SPROLIFERATION OF SURFACES → DELEUZE ANOTHER FOLD.
USER OF SURFACE?
LIMIT OF SURFACE?
SURFACE AS FRAME?

4 ST JAMES CHURCH
FORMER CHURCH. NOW GOLDSMITHS BUILDING
REAPPROPRIATION OF SPACE — RELIGIOUS SPACE TO ART SPACE. REUSABILITY OF SURFACE HIGHLIGHTS TRANSITORY NATURE OF SPACE.

5 BEN PIMLOTT BUILDING
FIRE ESCAPE
ART SCULPTURE ON SIDE OF BUILDING.
WALK TO TOP OF BUILDING FOR VIEW OF THE CITY. MICHEL DE CERTEAU — SUBTRACT OURSELVES FROM THE CITY CONTAIN THE CITY IN OUR GAZE. STREET SPACE IS ALL DIFFERENT LEVELS. CITY THROUGH TIME — CITY OF SPEEDS
BUILDING IS METAL AND GLASS. LOOK UP IN AWE AND WONDER.

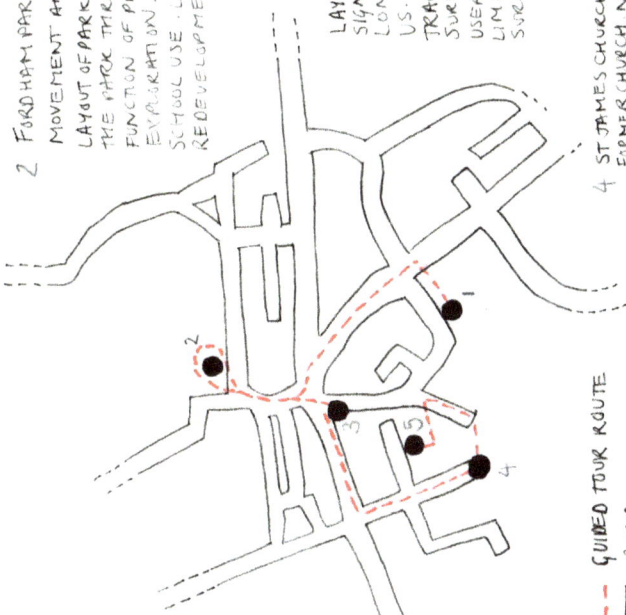

- - - - GUIDED TOUR ROUTE
———— ROAD
- - - - ROAD CONTINUES
● PLACE OF INTEREST

CITY POLITICAL WORKSHOP: DISCUSSING THE POLITICAL IN SPACE

Christian Berkes, Kenton Card & William Davis

Before reading below, ask yourself:

What is a political act?

Please write down your answer above.

Workshop as Anti-Form

The workshop's title speaks for itself. We want to discuss the open concepts of the 'city' and 'the political' in a space that remains open. Our goal is to get people into a certain kind of talking that is thematically focused, while structurally inclusive at the same time. Along the way, our vision is to explore the gap between action and thought, embodied here by an architectural practice and a theoretical reflection. Two videos became the starting point for our discussion: a trailer for the 'BMW Guggenheim Lab' in New York which was designed by the architects Atelier Bow-Wow and a short interview clip with the political geographer Erik Swyngedouw that introduces the terms 'politics' [*la politique*] and 'the political' [*le politique*].

The gap between the city and the political is a blind spot, which makes any integrative genealogy controversial and presumptuous, if not rash. We sought to create a temporary space and an instantaneous community to debate this gap. The conversation should confront professional and unprofessional, trained and untrained backgrounds. Today, we hear of multi, inter or transdisciplinary work everywhere. While people refer to such categories, we remain skeptical as to whether they confront the kernel of ideas within each department of knowledge. The City Political Workshop at the Centre for Cultural Studies (CCS) at Goldsmiths, University of London provides an *anti-form* – the gap between – to stage a dialogue in which people can confront each other's perspectives. A gap does not reinforce collective agreement, consensus, or baseless understanding of the others. The gap reveals the distance between. From within this negatively defined space, we can positively observe, confront, and articulate differing mindsets and new imaginations. At the same time we have to face the eventuality of getting lost in this in-between – which is a risk and an opportunity at the same time.

Quotes from the City Political Workshop on 26 June 2012

00:28:19
- Here is a consensus about dissensus. Suddenly we know what democracy is. I thought democracy was something that is supposed to be graspable, but now it's on a theoretical level. It's gonna be the same. There is something called 'radical heterogeneity', but who knows whether that even exists. How would you know it even exists? How could you actually build it? Is it demonstrable? It's just in the air. Academic overwriting.

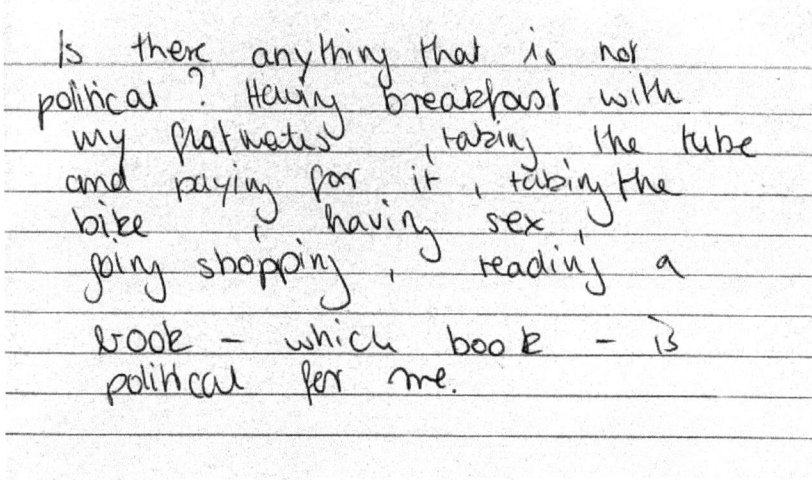

> Is there anything that is not political? Having breakfast with my flatmates, taking the tube and paying for it, taking the bike, having sex, going shopping, reading a book – which book – is political for me.

00:35:19
- A: I liked the lecture about rubbish we were talking about. Because the main thing to do is to relate to shit actually. Because there's a lot of it around and you have to devise ways of relating to that stuff. [...] So, you don't want to have anything to do with it, but it's all around. And we have to think about ways we might actually do that, to intact relationships not to our own radical outside but to our own shit. [...] So I have a much

more relational ethic than one of absolute difference and otherness, which I don't see as a new politics at all.

- B: What do you mean by rubbish?
- A: Oh, I don't know. I would leave that open. [...] It's all sorts of things conceivably social rubbish – people and things.

Negotiate a room, or space, in a way
that refuses what its architecture
(shape, structure, objects) wants you
to do

00:39:09

- This somehow relates to Kreuzberg (Berlin, Germany) as well. [...] The way something which is a bit rubbish, a bit dirty, a bit dodgy is somehow cool as well and is something you want to promote or keep like this. [...] But I thought it is interesting because people who somehow demonize gentrification very often make this claim.

a political act is any
act that raises the question
or refuses the continuation
of things as they are

00:41:47

- When they evicted the Occupy camps here in London or in the US it was always grounded in a health and safety or for the good of the people. I think that shows a lot of interesting ways in which the state can turn something which is a political thing into a sort of biological or sanitation thing. There is something like a 'sanitation of public space' that takes president over the actual public use of space.

00:46:04

- On what you were saying about the pop-up spaces and how they are sanctioned, etc. These temporary places like the Occupy movement – from the outside they looked a little like what you were describing. They looked like the perfect form of disobedience, this really lovely and grounded you know. It felt like it was exactly this permitted disobedience.

00:50:23

- It feels like there are two approaches to the political. You can just wait for it to come or you can try to find it everywhere, which is what tends to happen. People find that political moment everywhere and just read it into everything, which I find annoying.

00:54:47

- A: This relates back to a previous question: Are we searching for solutions or are we trying to find good questions? And solutions could be understood just as the opposite of problematization. [...]
- B: What these films show to me is that there is a sort of unbridgeable gap between *la politique* and *le politique*. There is no way to bridge that gap. In fact that contradiction is necessary in politics on a small scale, which

is part of urban politics. […] It's not about the question of answer or anything like that, solution or problematization. But it's about the power game and a very static situation, which they want to keep that way.

> Politics is the annihilation or recombination of a legal structure or system of codes.

01:01:27

- I don't know if there was demandlessnesses. I've heard this thing about they had no demands, which is exactly what they said about the youth in 2005 when the cars were burning in Paris' suburbs. And it's what they said, what Alain Badiou said and it's what Susan Buck-Morss said about the bombers. 'The bombers who destroyed the World Trade left no listed demands' they said. And that seems to me to be an awful misreading of what that event signifies: It is The – World – Trade – Centre.

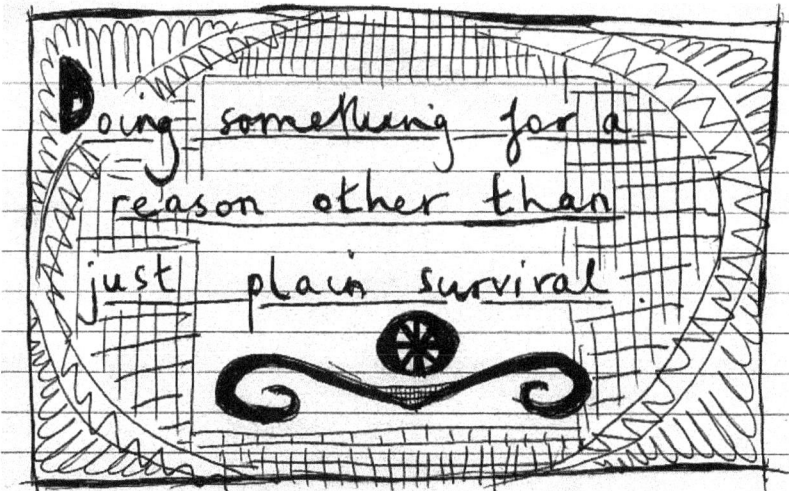

> Doing something for a reason other than just plain survival

- ~~myb~~ Express ourselves
- the right to express our opinion.

to act politically is to initiate
social change (eg. class
                 gender/sexuality
                 race
                 environment
                 disability)

01:14:26
- A little reflection on The Public School Berlin. Because I feel quite privileged, overeducated, missing a real grounding, for instance, in Berlin. It's mostly international people. I think one class has been in German.
- Not Turkish, not …
- No. But if you think about a free school where everybody can come and propose classes, which is sort of the starting point, it's extremely not. It's extremely exclusive, it's art classes, it's high theory classes. […] We're trying to be conscious about our own paradox of what we end up doing. Which is in a way to reproduce English as a hegemonic discourse language that is extremely exclusive.
- That really seems to be the first one to break.

ARE POLITICIANS
REDUNDANT?

CAN CITIES BE RUN
WITHOUT POLITICIANS?

01:22:52

- A: How do we figure out a language to communicate that isn't so incredibly academic and referential? This is a big question and a big resource. To me this seems to be something very fruitful and I don't want to say: All theory is shit and especially French theory.
- B: Can we write that down?
- A: But obviously it creates problems. Especially problems of colonisation of what the term the political means.

01:25:50

- There are all sorts of levels of participation in discussions. And they are getting lost very easily. I think that's a really valuable question.

01:29:00

- You can't have a conversation in not-normative languages. Because it wouldn't make any sense. But what I think we can do is have a conversation with a language under construction. [...] There is a lot to be said for the business of constructing a conversation and the skills that it requires.

SENTIMENTAL DESTRUCTION: THE LITERARY AVANT-GARDE AND THE RUINATION OF SPACE IN THE FIRST SOVIET DECADE

Maxwell Anley

The English language publication of Boris Groys' *The Total Art of Stalinism* inscribed power ontologies into accounts of the Russian avant-garde. Groys identifies the will to power in all manifestations of the avant-garde, inflecting all attempts to configure reality in aesthetic terms through the act of life-creation [*zhiznetvorchestvo*] (Groys, 1992). Groys' thesis is still controversial, due to his insistence on a shared power ontology between non-conformist – even proto-dissident – members of the pre-Stalinist cultural community and the murderous onslaught of High Stalinism, with its show trials and the Ezhovshchina of 1937. This conflation of the pre- and post- Cultural Revolutionary artistic praxis threatens an equally monolithic account of artistic life in the U.S.S.R: ethically superior dissidentism versus conformism. To stoop to a nominal, one line history of the great men (and women) of Soviet Culture, Zamiatin, Bulgakov, Akhmatova, Mandel′shtam, Tsvetaeva, Mayakovsky, Solzhenitsyn, Pasternak, Sinyavskii and Danil, are all 'victims' in conventionalized accounts of the Soviet state apparatus and, arguably, the hopelessly reductive account of cultural history of *pro* and *contra* perpetuated in the West.

With this paper, I use the concept of the production of space to challenge the 'dissident' / 'conformist' binary account of Soviet Culture; and attempt a trajectory that maintains a more nuanced account of power ontologies in cultural life than the reductive will-to-power offered by Groys. I address the production of space by two non-conformist figures in the post-revolutionary literary avant-garde: reluctant OBERIU member Konstantin Vaginov; and staunch Formalist Viktor Shklovsky. I will focus on their depiction of late Russian and early Soviet modernity as a space of ruin and collapse. The topos of ruination, where an authentic cultural essence lies in a state of ruin in a debased present, is doubtless a potent device with which to lament the collapse of a previous cultural order and adopt a stance of resistance to contemporary reality. However, it is precisely this 'dissident' ruination of Bolshevik reality and its associated position in the cultural field which I seek to problematize here. As such, it is important to highlight two key tenets of how I determine the production of space. Firstly, in my examination of ruination, I consider the representations of material reality in texts as active components in the (onto)logic of reality and its future orientation. The production of space is therefore understood to be subject to a dialectic between the material and its logical cognition in the ground of modernity.[1] Secondly, I use Bourdieu's spatial concepts of the field and habitus to account for the necessity of power in cultural production, thereby problematizing both the purely 'wilful' account of power-in-culture found in Groys and the 'positions' entailed by the conformist / dissident binary paradigm of Soviet cultural life (Bourdieu, 1993).

I. Vaginov and ruination

Around the time of the onset of the Cultural Revolution, Konstantin Vaginov published his first novel *The Goat Song*. It depicts a group of the old-order cultural intelligentsia struggling to adapt to life in what they perceive to be the ruinous aftermath of the Bolshevik Revolution. Fearful of the advent of a destructive new culture, the group seeks to preserve the values of classical culture in the hope that classicism will be reborn and perpetuated in a glorious future epoch. The novel does not merely depict a material existence of ruin, but conveys how culture itself is in a state of collapse and old forms have lost relevance. Throughout this 'narrative', various characters commit suicide in despair or die highly symbolic deaths, only subsequently to reappear and resume their roles, as if to affirm that such grand acts of symbolism have lost their validity in the debased ruin-present of the novel. The narrator maintains an uncertain, fragile presence throughout the novel. He talks with his characters, inviting them to dinner and discussing the fate of culture and their fictional representations. The novel's title alludes to the Greek etymology of tragedy, and can be translated either as 'Satyr Chorus' or 'The Goat Song'. Either way, the title foregrounds the absurd notion of a chorus of singing goats, and contains none of the emotional gravity and catharsis found in classical Greek tragedy.

The pervasive sense of the ruination of material reality and cultural forms is evident in the two prefaces to the novel. The first reads:

---

[1] The key influence here is Henri Lefebvre, however I do not accept how he allocates textual sources (as opposed to material structures) a subordinate role in the production of space. See Lefebvre (1991).

Preface

Pronounced by an author who is appearing on the threshold of the...book

For some time now, I've felt that Petersburg has been daubed in a greenish colour, flickering and flashing, a ghastly phosphorescent colour. On walls, in houses and in souls a green flame trembles, sly and sniggering. The flame flickers – it is not Petr Petrovich in front of you but a slimy reptile. The flame leaps up – and you yourself have become worse than a reptile. It is not people that walk the streets: you peer under a hat – a snake's head; you squint at an old woman – a toad sits, its fat belly trembling. And the young, each with their own obsession: an engineer craves to listen to Hawaiian music; a student – a striking suicide stunt; a schoolboy – to raise a child, and thereby demonstrate his masculinity. You pop into a shop – a former general stands behind the counter, smiling artificially; you go into a museum – the guide knows that he is lying, but still continues to lie... I don't love Petersburg. My dream is over. (Vaginov, 2008)

Over the page, and the second preface reads:

Preface

Pronounced by an author who has appeared in the middle of the book.

Now Petersburg is no more. There is Leningrad; but Leningrad does not concern us. The author is an undertaker by profession, and not a master cradlemaker. Show him a coffin – he'll give it a tap and he'll know from what material it was made, how long ago, by which master, and he'll even remember the predecessors of the deceased. The author has been making a small coffin for twenty-seven years of his life. He's terribly busy. But don't think that he's making a coffin with some aim in mind – it's just a passion of his. He raises his nose – and catches the stink of a corpse;

that means you need a coffin. And the author loves all
of his deceased, he walks with them in life, shaking
their hands and chatting with them, slowly preparing
the planks, buying a few nails and, should the chance
arise, some lace. (Vaginov, 2008)

On the simplest of levels, the pervasive atmosphere of doom and ruination can
be figured as an oppositional response to the Revolution of 1917, and has been
widely understood as such in critical accounts of the novel to date (Shepherd,
1991). I will briefly pursue this 'dissident' reading here before questioning its
tenability.

The flickering light, which covers Petersburg in a sickly green patina, evokes
a disturbing atmosphere of unease where the Revolution has corrupted essence
and rendered appearances deceptive. In the inverted, post-Revolutionary social
order where a former general stands smiling artificially behind a shop counter,
the youth of Petersburg can only harbour their aspirations internally, and do
not express them. Perhaps most disturbing of all for the author-narrator is the
lying museum guide, implying that Bolshevik cultural hegemony has advanced
into the museum and is perpetuating false-truths about culture. In the second
preface, the Bolshevik order has advanced out of the museum and written itself
onto the city-text of Petersburg in the act of re-naming the city after its deceased
leader. In an ironic inversion of the avant-garde telos of *zhiznetvorchestvo*, the
author's profession is likened to that of a coffin maker or undertaker. The creative act of writing has become moribund in the tragic ontology, and any possible
dialogue with literary heroes can only end in death.

It is worth noting that, in accordance with this limited reading of the prefaces which I am pursuing here, it is not just the physical space of post-Revolutionary Petersburg which is in a state of ruin and destruction. The first preface
declares itself to be written by an author who is appearing on the threshold of
a book; the second is written by an author who has appeared in the 'middle' of
the book. We might expect a second preface to be written some years after the
book's initial publication when the author has had a chance to reflect on his or
her opinion of the book, and whether it is still valuable as a work of art. Here
this spatio-temporal frame has been drastically accelerated and foreshortened
by the pace of events in the aftermath of the Revolution. With the re-naming of
the city, the former capital of imperial culture, it is as if the fictional space of the
novel has come under intense compression and is warping and distorting.

In accordance with this simplistic reading of Vaginov's 'dissident' production of post-Revolutionary ruin-space, it would be all too easy to locate the novel amongst discourses of ruination and the authentic. Such discourses locate
the authentic in the past, anterior to the debased cultural environment of the
present (Huyssen, 2010). The debased present of the novel, complete with its

fractured sense of self, frustrated ambition, artificial emotion and death, would therefore denote that (early Soviet) modernity which 'fosters the growth of disciplinary power and surveillance, the fragmentation of the subject, the capacity for destruction and mass death on a scale never before possible, and the creation of new ways of subjugating people and controlling society' (Presner, 2010). In accordance with this discourse of authenticity, the lone figure of the dissident artist-intellectual produced here occupies a position at the ultimate periphery of cultural space, distant from the oppressive centre and its power apparatus. In the novel the characters retreat to a 'tower', a rented Dacha a short distance away from Petersburg / Leningrad, which they believe will serve as a fortress in which they can preserve the values of classical culture from the degraded reality of the post-Revolutionary present.

This production of centre and periphery in ruin-space is highly ambiguous in terms of how we are to configure power trajectories within the cultural field. In line with the 'dissident' reading of the novel, the refusal to participate in the degraded cultural centre and instead retreat to the margins of cultural space reads like a refusal of Groysian will-to-power, and a denial of the early Soviet habitus. Yet the characters themselves are ironically depicted as being highly ambitious, undertaking their retreat precisely because they believe it will bring the rewards of habitus once classical culture is reborn. In a ruthless parody of precisely that will-to-power identified by Groys, Vaginov depicts the character Teptelkin sitting in an apartment full of classical kitsch. Teptelkin daydreams of a future summons from a triumphant Mussolini, requesting that he participate in the creation of a new language for the re-born empire of Rome. Vaginov, I suggest, is aware that this refusal to participate in the cultural centre, and the accompanying ruination of space, is an attempt to create a kind of inverse habitus, where the trump cards are not short-term institutional success and material gain, but total loss, suffering and ruin. The desired destruction of the post-Revolutionary present is therefore equally attributable to the values of the old, pre-Revolutionary order and not the tenets of Bolshevism *per se*. In order to assert its power trajectory, the 'old-order' depicted in the novel desire their own collapse and ruin to assume ultimate power in the cultural field. The prefaces to the novel should therefore be understood as a *parody* of earnest predictions of ruin and collapse in the cultural field and their concomitant power trajectory.

That most critical accounts should ignore this readily apparent irony and take the prefaces at face value is surprising, particularly given the generic production of space in the literature of the so-called Petersburg theme up to the Revolution. Much of the content in both prefaces refracts and perpetuates the generic structures of the Petersburg theme which figure in the work of Pushkin, Dostoevsky, Gogol, Bely and others. In broad terms, this topos can be understood as two related dialectics: progress and ruin; and the rational and terror. Peter the Great, perhaps Russia's first modernist, attempted to reconfigure Russian identity with a window onto Europe by building a new city in his own image, thereby affecting a fundamental shift in the production of space through the construction of a 'Venice of the North' along the rational norms of enlightenment thought. This early volitional act of *zhiznetvorchestvo* provoked highly ambiguous responses in Russian literature, and was understood as an arrogant act of man's superiority before nature and God, inviting nemesis of apocalyptic proportions. The articulation of sinister, synechdochal Gogolian imagery in the urban environment of the first preface economically perpetuates these generic norms. The analogy of the author to the undertaker tapping his materials is more ambiguous, possibly a reference to Pushkin's prose work of the same name; or, more likely, a nod towards Chekhov's early short story *A Dreadful Night*, where a narrator suffers after attending a spiritualist séance where he perceives the apparition of the rationalist philosopher Spinoza. Warned by Spinoza of his immanent death, the narrator perceives coffins in every apartment he visits one evening. The re-naming of Petersburg to Leningrad, the ruthless reconfiguration of a national cultural identity, and the irrational engendered by the rational are all topoi which assert continuity from Russian into early Soviet modernity. To lament the collapse and manifest redundancy of the 'old' pre-Revolutionary order in the face of the 'new' order of Socialism is to miss these apparent continuities with the early Soviet epoch, complete with the re-naming of the city after the Revolutionary leader.

II. Shklovsky and Ruination

> How did I wind up at the front? Lenin arrived. There were Bolsheviks in the motor pools of the division; they offered Lenin an armoured car for the trip from the station to the Kshensinskaya Palace, which our unit had taken over for quarters. A certain part of the division was decisively for the Bolsheviks. I was then on the division committee and, with my school, represented the wing of the division that wanted to continue the war (Shklovsky, 2004).

In the second preface to *The Goat Song*, the re-naming of Petersburg after the deceased leader signals the increasingly peripheral status of the narrator. In this early passage taken from Viktor Shklovsky's autobiographical novel *A Sentimental Journey*, the arrival of Lenin in Revolutionary Petersburg initiates Shklovsky's journey to the periphery of cultural space. Shklovsky recounts a trip in an armoured car to the front line in World War I. In direct disagreement with Lenin, Shklovsky attempted to persuade the Soviet army to continue fighting in the War. This journey to the periphery and beyond produces an early Soviet space pervaded by ruin, desolation and despair.

Buildings' walls have completely washed away leaving only their roofs, cars are frequently stuck in the mud, their wheels spinning; the army undertake suicidal missions and many are unnecessarily slaughtered in friendly fire. In this and his other hybrid critical-autobiographical works *Knight's Move, Zoo... or Letters not About Love* and *The Third Factory*, Shklovsky produces a defamiliarized Russian national space in the aftermath of the Revolution, a landscape of famine and deprivation. The great and the good of Russian culture queue for their basic provisions, potentially, we might imagine, being served by the former general working behind the shop counter of Vaginov's preface to *The Goat Song*. In 1922 Shklovsky was forced even further into the periphery of Soviet cultural space, fleeing into exile in Berlin due to suspicions of his counter Revolutionary activity before his return a little over a year later.

Shklovsky's peripheral 'dissident' status in the early Soviet cultural field is, however, less attributable to any counter Revolutionary activity or his efforts to prolong Russia's involvement in the war. He was prepared to admit the short-comings of his earlier ideological convictions, writing in his postscript to *Zoo...*: 'The whole thing is simple—straightforward and elementary. Down with Imperialism. Long live the brotherhood of peoples. If one must perish, let it be for that. Was it conceivably for this piece of knowledge that I journeyed so far?' (Shklovsky, 2001). Shklovsky's trajectory away from the arrival of Lenin to the periphery of ruin, exile and subsequent return lead him to appreciate the wisdom of Marxist-Leninism in terms of imperialism. The following passage from *A Sentimental Journey* produces a space of colonial antagonisms in Russian occupied Persia. With its defamiliarized depiction of capital, it might have served as an absurd addendum to Lenin's chapters on banks and finance in *Imperialism: The Last Stage of Capitalism*:

> Then a new difficulty arose. It's impossible to imagine anything more capricious than the rate of exchange in Persia. Small silver coins had one rate of exchange, roubles another. Even gold had its own rate of exchange—not according to weight, but where it was minted, so that one weight of gold in Turkish lira was worth much more than the same weight in Russian pieces. Small Russian banknotes had their own rate of exchange. Hundred-rouble notes and five-hundred-rouble notes had still another rate of exchange, the thousand-rouble note showing the Duma another, the 'kerenkas,' just issued by the Provisional government, still another. Moreover, the rate for the Russian rouble would change literally twice a day, depending on the latest information from Tabriz. No need to say that the Russian bank in Tabriz wouldn't take Russian money. The situation got to be such that at each change in value, the soldier felt that he'd been cheated—and, in fact, he had been.
>
> The minute silver was handed out, the soldiers all rushed to change it into roubles, which they would take back to Russia. The bankers (sarafs) would momentarily inflate the rouble by fifteen kopeks (shai) and more, and the soldiers, feeling resentful, would stage a series of pogroms. The pogroms, however, were constant' (Shklovsky, 2004).

Like Vaginov's ambivalent dialectical modernity of progress and ruin, the 'dissident' Shklovsky clearly does not produce this cultural ruin-space in order to preserve the essence of some noble cultural order. He is equally liable to lament the sheer desolation of modern imperialist warfare and the alienation of technological innovations such as the telephone, as he is clearly in thrall to the dynamic power of the motorcar, a 1000 Break Horse Power diesel engine and the machine gun. Whilst undeniably damaged goods due to his own counter revolutionary activity, Shklovsky's peripheral status in the Soviet cultural field was largely due to his insistence on the 'straightforward' and 'elementary' truths of his Russian Formalist criticism: art is entirely separate from ideology and life.

Shklovsky's witty arguments in defence of the Formalist position, and the particularly fierce struggle with proponents of Marxist-materialist critique – where the life / art relationship is entirely subject to that crudest of dialectics, the base / superstructure determinism – is ground that has been well covered elsewhere, and is not worth repeating here (Erlich, 1965). Of greater relevance for the current discussion is how this fierce struggle over methodology in literary praxis produces particular positions in the early Soviet cultural field; positions which undeniably launch trajectories towards power. As a staunch defender of the autonomy of artistic structures from life and ideology, Shklovsky is an unsuitable candidate for Groys's avant-garde that sought power through *zhiznetvorchestvo*. By insisting on the artist's contingency upon the immanent formal laws of the work of art, even to the point where artistic volition is thwarted precisely due to the terms of immanent law, Shklovsky severely limits any possible will-to-power through art. Yet, as Bourdieu notes, the insistence on art's autonomy is itself productive of a particular sociology, serving as a methodological wager upon prestige and habitus in the fields of culture and power (Bourdieu, 1993).

Despite his likely protestations to the contrary, Shklovsky's production of a Revolutionary ruin-space in *A Sentimental Journey* and his other works is a crucial component of his trajectory towards habitus. Shklovsky consistently interrupts his narrative of hopeless warfare at the front with recollections of how he and his Formalist colleagues did not abandon their meetings and publications in the face of similar hardship and desolation at the periphery of cultural life. Like the intellectuals and artists parodied in Vaginov's *The Goat Song*, Shklovsky is so convinced of the value of his knowledge that he is intent to preserve it even in the face of suffering and ruin. However, unlike those characters, Shklovsky does not will the demise of his cultural values in order that they be reborn again and assume the spoils of habitus. For Shklovsky, suffering at the periphery of cultural space serves to validate the fundamental truth content of his Formalist method, but it stops short of intending culture's demise in order to assert that truth.

Beginning? Forever Ending?

The net result of Vaginov's parody is the production of an open post-Revolutionary space, where cultural forms refract the innovations, continuations and contingencies that pervade modernity. The insistence on attributing a specific symbolic form to a given epochal essence is unsustainable, a tragic act doomed to recognise its own futility. Rather than read Vaginov as a dissident on the eve of high-Stalinist Socialist Realism, or the nostalgic gravedigger of the old cultural order, *The Goat Song* retrospectively offers many possible new beginnings and trajectories for Soviet culture. Shklovsky is not so optimistic. Arguably, the modernity which grounds Shklovsky's journey is analogous to that of Adorno's highly pessimistic *Minima Moralia*, where production always results in collapse and decline, regardless of any progressive intention and the realization of imperialism's inherent flaws (Adorno, 2005). Shklovsky accepts the wisdom of Lenin's attack on imperialism and the value of the brotherhood of man, but that is not to say that he believes in their eventual triumph. It is more likely that people will die the worthwhile death fighting for this cause than see its eventual realization.

References

Adorno, T. 2005. *Minima Moralia: Reflections on a Damaged Life*. London and New York, NY. Verso.

Bourdieu, P. 1993. *The Field of Cultural Production*. Edited by Randal Johnson. Cambridge. Polity.

Erlich, V. 1965. *Russian Formalism: History / Doctrine*. The Hague. Moulton.

Groys, B. 1992. *The Total Art of Stalinism: Avant-garde, Aesthetic Dictatorship and Beyond*. Translated by Charles Rougle. Princeton, NJ. Princeton University Press.

Hell, J. and Schönle, A. (eds). 2010. *The Ruins of Modernity*. Durham, NC and London. Duke University Press.

Lefebvre, H. 1991. *The Production of Space*. Translated by Donald Nicholson Smith. Oxford. Blackwell.

Lenin, V. 1928. *Imperialism: The Last Stage of Capitalism*. London. Dorrit Press.

Shepherd, D. 1991. *Beyond Metafiction: Self-Consciousness in Soviet Literature*. Oxford. Clarendon Press.

Shklovsky, V. 2005. *Knight's Move*. Translated by Richard Sheldon. Champaign, IL. Dalkey Archive.

_____ . 2004. *A Sentimental Journey: Memoirs, 1917-1922*. Translated by Richard Sheldon. Champaign, IL. Dalkey Archive.

_____ . 2002. *Third Factory*. Translated by Richard Sheldon. Champaign, IL. Dalkey Archive.

_____ . 2001. *Zoo, Or Letters not about Love*. Translated by Richard Sheldon. Champaign, IL. Dalkey Archive.

Vaginov, K. 2008. *Kozlinaia pesn'*. Moscow. Eksmo.

INLAND DRIFT: A PHOTO ESSAY

Jamal Aridi

You start from somewhere. Time and presence are demanded but in the process it isn't very hard to find oneself going nowhere. What surfaces as aspects of everyday life will not always call us out on our route but may become a metaphor for caving when the cracks begin to appear. Caving as the vertical axis for relations on the ground. The spectacular however prevents showing cracks. The seams must be rounded and edges planned. And if they do appear then they must be well accounted for.

The journey begins in London. Surrey Quays all too aware of its own transience. The arrows on the billboard ahead of the train station won't lead to California and the sun may not rise again for days. Luckily there is a Wetherspoons across the road.

Moving south to New Cross. The peeled sign heralds the world ahead and its relations whilst connecting it globally. Charlottenburg, being one of the poshest parts of Berlin, forms an unusual pairing with New Cross. Think of Wittgenstein and Jessie J announcing they are twinsies.

Which takes us to Berlin, the Bauhaus Museum.

The plaque reads:

Extemporal Zone
Representation of
Eternity
In every moment
uchronia before utopia.

If I remember correctly…

This presentation is screened on loop at Beirut's Zaitunay Bay, whose lined restaurants make for a faker version of the South Bank, informing us against the company developing the marina. This frame reads: UNBELIEVABLE! YET TRUE

Could these Roman ruins under the Beyrouth Souks mall be an example of uchronia?

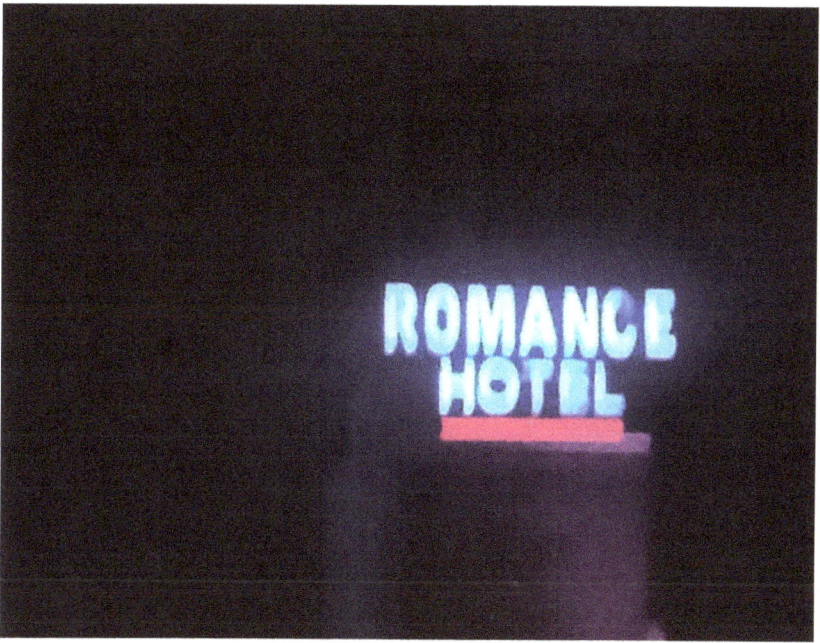

What does an implemented uchronia look like? The red light district north of Beirut, relocated from the city centre some time ago. A time for liberating pleasure and fantasy that exposes the banality of everyday time.

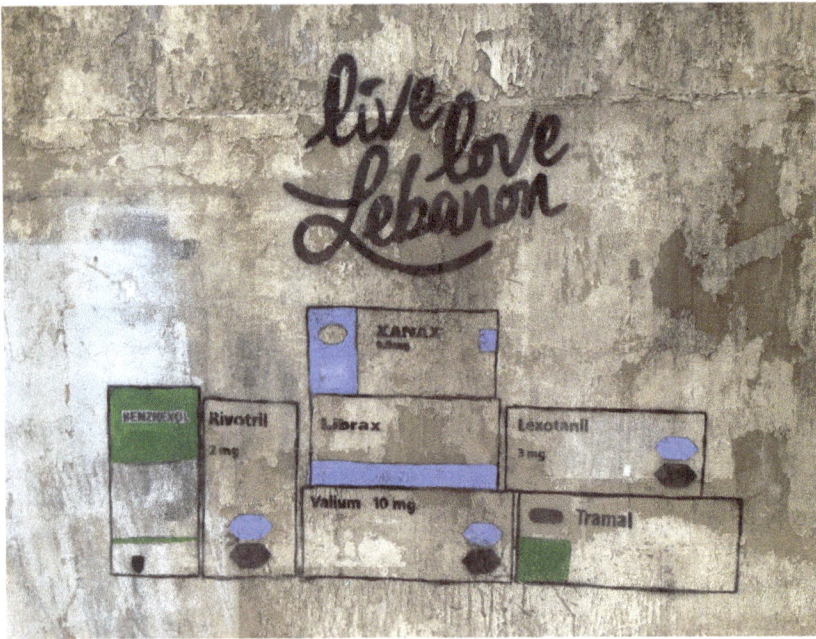

On a wall close to a major hospital in the city's heart this stencil advertises the most popular high street drugs.

No hustling please.

All that travel has induced vertigo.

Have I been here before? I am at an irreproducible atemporal nowhere.

How does one account for such a time?

This ad for jet lag pills on the airport train may be just what I need to consume.

JAMAL ARIDI

ANTIPODEAN TOPOLOGIES

Argos Aotearoa

... Waters ...

A brick sewer in Queen Street, Auckland City, New Zealand. Public Domain. Available: https://commons.wikimedia.org/wiki/File:Queen_Street_Brick_Cover_Tunnel.jpg

It makes a difference where you begin. Above ground or below, in flowing traffic or in stagnant ponds.

Queen Street, the congested heart of sprawling Tāmaki Makaurau (Auckland), has the difference written across and beneath it.[1] The Auckland Council, a recent merger of seven formerly autonomous district councils and twenty-one local boards (such that it is now the largest council in Australasia), has a strong-

---

[1] For the artwork that inspired this section, see *Horotiu* by Local Time. Accessed at www.local-time.net/local-time-horotiu/ (11 November 2013).

ly metonymic sense of its own authority. It speaks the legion voice of Auckland itself, and of late it has been uttering a new chant: that Auckland should be 'the world's most liveable city'.

This is perhaps a humble aim, if 'liveable' is understood in the sense of a minimal endurability, a fitness for bare life - a baseline ability to be lived or lived-in. It seems the creators of the otherwise obscure Liveable Cities Index interpreted it this way: the Index was originally devised as a tool to enable employers to assign hardship benefits for relocated employees. Moving to Auckland in 2011 or 2012 granted one the third lowest hardship allowance in the world. Twice we won bronze in the rankings, through some strange algorithmicising of indicators: 'environment', 'culture', 'ease of doing business' (Greenway, 2010). And for our Supercity with its freshly-minted Unitary Plan, the slipperiness of the term 'liveable' - its aspirational-yet-already-achievedness - makes it a perfect flag to fly, an emblem of the empty 'one' that it claims we are.

As the Supercity understands it, to live well means to clean up the clogged veins of Tāmaki Makaurau, enabling the smooth flow of both people and capital. And it is true that our transportation system is perhaps our decisive flaw in the 'liveable cities' stakes, forever precluding the prospect of gold. Space above ground is already maximally threaded with motorways and rail, settled in tar wherever volcanic hills do not protrude. It had been imagined by the planners that below ground, in what seem untapped depths of soft earth marbled with bore-able basalt and old lava courses, we might carve out an endless matrix of tunnels. But in 2011, the proposed central Auckland rail link - which would run beneath the Central Business District, roughly down the length of Queen Street, towards the sea - was momentarily blocked when Glen Wilcox, who sits on the Council's Māori advisory board, raised a question. 'What's being done about the taniwha Horotiu who lives just outside here?' he asked, pointing out 'that tunnel will be going right through his rohe.'[2]

*

Taniwha assume various guises and their appearance may be indexed in various ways. As Wilcox puts it, 'as kaitiaki, or guardians, they protect people, but they also get up and bite you if they do not like what you are doing' (Wilcox, cited in Field, 2011). Horotiu is the namesake of Waihorotiu, the stream on top of whose once-swampy ground Queen Street now sits. Children used to fish for eel along the stream's fern-clad banks and from the time of European arrival in the early nineteenth century, tide-permitting, trading schooners could be taken as far as the Bank of New Zealand and rowboats right up to the waterfall at Victoria Street (Jefferson, 1996). Stabilising such a swampy area in the interests of

---

[2] Rohe is generally translated as a boundary or territory of an iwi (tribe) or hapū (subtribe).

urban development was difficult, however, and eventually it became a fetid canal named after Charles Ligar, whose inept design meant that it harboured raw sewage from the nearby settlements. It took until 1873 for the Ligar Canal to be covered up completely, a new brick sewer keeping the waste of a fast-expanding Pākehā population out of sight, under the pavement.[3]

*

Wilcox's question goes unanswered and, for the most part, unheard. In the council meeting, it was met with 'scattered laughter'. In the press, it was made into an object of bad jokes ('who is the *real* taniwha here?' (Twyford, 2011)) and straight-faced racism (see for example Round, 2011). Horotiu, in turn, became assimilated into various Pākehā scripts, interpreted as an expression of ecological awareness or of the incomplete inclusion of Ngāti Whātua, the original inhabitants and guardians of the area, in the council's consultation process. But when heard in and on its own terms, Wilcox's question forces us to start differently, or again; to rethink ourselves in relation to another map of this place. Rather than acting to flatten space into its singular, present iteration, erasing extraneous shadows and folds of the land, this map is a tracing of deep geological fissures: a record of eruption, burial, and sedimentation compressed over generations. It is a map of plural planes to be conceived at once, of lives ligatured to those that have come before. The waters of Horotiu run deep beneath the CBD. We can drink from them today at Te Waiariki, the spring that flows from an ivy-lined wall in the parking lot of the University of Auckland Law School. One doesn't see people lining up with buckets nowadays, but this spring served as a significant water supply for both Māori and Pākehā during the drought in the 1840s, and was piped down to what was then Official Bay so that boats could refill their barrels.

Waihorotiu tends to attract the past tense, as though sealing a road with tar can dry up the water that moves beneath it. But if we choose our words differently, things change. The waters of Horotiu continue to run and give shape to the furrows and ridges of our city, and Horotiu continues to live beneath the streets of the CBD. To speak this way is to ensure that the temporal predicate of 'the present' (what's now) necessarily also contains what has come before, and that its spatial predicate (what's here) is rendered not according to a 'clean-slate' capitalist common sense, but rather as being caught up in the web of intensities, breaks and slowly-unfurling events that have preceded it.

Only this way can history move beyond its minimal claim for 'heritage',

---

[3] Pākehā, which has associations with being 'pale-skinned' refers to the originally Anglo-European non-Māori population, but can be taken to include all non-Māori New Zealanders. Many non-Māori, however, refuse this pan-Māori word for themselves, because it denominates them in view of Māori, preferring 'New Zealander' or 'Kiwi'.

which speaks of the always-deficient consolation (inheritance) for the one that is (from the root *heir*) 'empty, left behind'. Through heritage sites, history is acknowledged while foreclosed, peppered across place as quaint attraction or cultural spice, and as such, one can choose or choose not to engage with it. History made optional - as reflected in calls made by the recently-formed 'Pakeha Party' for 'equality for *all* New Zealand races [by] moving together into the future as one'[4] - follows a liberal common sense where the symbolic rights of the individual generate an abstraction from the worlds in which these rights are, presumably, to be realised. As Avril Bell tells us, for Pākehā to divest themselves of their history, they must imagine their rebirth from the *land itself*, as '"born again" New Zealanders, disowning their parents and imagining themselves adopted' (Bell, cited in Mikaere, 2011:100).

Te Waiariki indexes the waters of Horotiu beneath it, just as Wilcox's question of the taniwha indexes other ways of being in and understanding our place. But despite their popular portrayal as such, these are not mere relics of the past. The taniwha Horotiu lives beneath the streets of a city whose colonisation finds ever new ways to rejuvenate itself, not least through partitioning the metropolitan area along lines of finance capital, with predictable disregard for the communities that cut across these.[5] Horotiu shows us that we always stand before our past - facing it, answerable to it - because we are its trace, a sign of its presence

Speaking of the link between whakapapa (genealogy) and taonga (treasures), Ani Mikaere reminds us that 'we are, after all, the physical manifestation of our forebears, ngā kanohi ora o rātou mā, and so we should take care of ourselves accordingly' (Mikaere, 2011: 298).[6] Care for the present starts with an obligation to these forebears, and to a past that continues to flow within - and at times block - the spaces of our city and selves. An obligation: literally, a binding-together. On this basis, we are called upon to strive for more than a teeth-gritting, just-bear-able liveability, and an understanding of what blocks this place, rather than the ever more efficient ways to make it flow.

*

---

[4] Available http://www.facebook.com/ThePakehaParty. Accessed 11/11/2013.

[5] In recent years, Housing New Zealand has been engaged in the forced removal of a number of state houses in Glen Innes, now deemed a seaside suburb with high market potential, so as to on-sell their plots to developers. Some of the families affected, largely Māori or Pacific, have lived in the community for more than fifty years. Four elderly members of the community have died since hearing the news of their eviction, and countless others (including MP Hone Harawira) have been injured and arrested during protests against the removals.

[6] 'Ngā kanohi ora o rātou mā' is translated by Mikaere elsewhere as 'the living faces of those who have gone on before us' (Mikaere, 2002).

Photograph by Anna Boswell with permission.

If what used to be the University of Auckland law school and library is now occupied only by the library, the space it takes up is still very much a matter of law and knowledge. How local behaviour is organised in terms of the law is what local people 'know', and the university is a privileged and self-appointed repository and regulator of this knowledge.

A 'police order' of intelligence, or a 'distribution of the sensible' (Rancière, 2006) - what it is possible to perceive, say, do - could hardly find better illustration than in the Albert barracks wall, which today runs adjacent to the library. This wall was constructed from local basalt rock in the mid-1840s, almost four decades before the founding of the university. Concretising the perceived military threat posed to Auckland's Pākehā residents by northern Māori, it demarcates, or quite literally circumscribes, a settler presence and identity whose predicate is an historical 'state of emergency'. At the time when it was raised, the barracks was large enough to house Auckland's fledgling settler population. In the centre of the compound stood Government House, since gone up in fire, rebuilt, and repurposed as the university staff commons furnished with portrait galleries, leather armchairs and an extensive whiskey list. This building endures as both site and sign of the exceptional sovereignty of settler law, conditioned to this day on its withdrawal from anyone who threatens the 'New Zealand' of New Zealand's second peoples (the paramilitary invasion in 2007 of the historical territory of Tūhoe, a tribe with long-stated ambitions to be self-sovereign, is a case in point).

While you couldn't really say that the remnant section of the barracks wall is actively being remembered by the official machineries of settler memory, over time it has come to be heritage-protected. It is, no doubt, viewed by current university management as an obstruction, since it cuts across 'valuable' real-estate in the heart of the city campus, and since its narrow aperture often causes bottlenecks, impeding the smooth flow of the staff members and student 'customers' who line up on either side of the payroll. Pedagogically speaking, however, the superimposition of the university campus over the site of the barracks seems particularly apt, since a settler place must - necessarily, always - strive to teach its public how to be here, or how to imagine being here. It is imperative that the residents of a 'new' country, as well as the very idea of such a place, be secured as such if they are to have a future. New Zealand public life, then, is instituted through certain spatial and physical orientations, and the sense of self and place that these supply. The barracks indicate that the 'public' of the country-to-be - in the first instance, residents of colonial Auckland - is constructed in the light of military emergency. Inscribing a line of defence, such a landmark writes the new country into being. As a surface ridge of scar tissue, the barracks reminds us, too, of the 'correctional' basis of life in a new world, where space is taken, broken in, wounded. Such rectographic over-writing, which seeks to replace, displace and erase an existing Indigenous sensible order in order to secure both the land and the ongoing grounds of its second occupation, is intrinsic to the take-over and make-over culture of settlement.

If law and wall indicate how space here is occupied, the nearby bronze sculpture by Michael Parekowhai bespeaks this circumscription. The object of bemused curiosity since it appeared, this severe-looking figure can be taken to be an important public figure, much like the statue of the former Auckland mayor, Sir Dove Myer Robinson, which stands down the hill in the central city Aotea Square. Disarmingly, though, the feet of Parekowhai's guardian-like figure rest on turf rather than on an elevated plinth. Closer inspection reveals this figure to be a security guard, a sign, perhaps, of the greater walled campus - a newly-enhanced site of management anxiety and securitisation, given an embattled Vice Chancellor and militant student and union movements. Binding together past and present concerns with security and settler futurity in a new country, the guard patrols the barracks wall, behind which looms the library, itself a fortress or stronghold for all the 'knowledge' that is safeguarded within it. This tableau seems to mark out a deep-seated fear, as if it responds to an official order for special protection - from a longer history of the place, from other knowledges and ways of organising and thinking about life, from the very waterways upon which the campus sits.

*

The grounds of knowledge are inseparable from the grounds of place or what, in New Zealand, is called 'settlement'. But we refuse the idea that local grounds are in any way settled (politically, culturally, historically, geo-physically). Excavation of this image - its spatialising of the built environment, its inscription of land - throws up the constitutive precarity of settler inhabitation in a place with a longer history. The New Zealand public is predicated on self-dissimilarity, an un-wholeness or brokenness which is really a matter of internal rupture, or *different differences*. Whatever it is that the memory-machinery of the local history industry tells us, and however hard the settler state tries to unite its citizens as the corporate body proclaimed by Lieutenant-Governor William Hobson at the first signing of the Treaty of Waitangi in February 1840 ('He iwi tahi tatou' - 'We are now one people'), New Zealanders today are not altogether the 'better Britons' of the nineteenth century. The public of the barracks wall is fractured by the uncommon commons of Māori. Periodic assertions of this Indigenous commons - through claims to land, water, flora and fauna, for instance, whose attributes Māori peoples take to be the substance of their own self-sovereignty, or First law[7] - still spark a collective wagon-circling panic in the majority settler population.

The word Māori, which means 'ordinary' or 'common', reminds us of a time before the first peoples of this place became, in their own lands, the exotic strangers of foreigners' gaze - before 'they' were constituted as an administrative collective in the interests of expediting European take-over. If Māori suggest dissimilar grounds of inhabitation that bespeak a constitutional deficit, then local security and surveillance are all the more needed (the 'five eyes' surveillance network of Britain, the US, Canada, Australia and New Zealand is united, of course, by its members' own shared histories of occupying other peoples' countries). Prior Māori ground also suggests a double or deeper commons of which anti-capitalist movements must take cognisance if they are to avoid re-taking space and re-instigating Indigenous injury. We suggest that the university's own grounds are as good a starting point as any for investigating what it might mean to 'occupy' ground that is broken in these kinds of ways - indeed, for investigating the very notion of the grounds of knowledge.

---

[7] Ani Mikaere uses this phrase throughout *Colonising Myths – Māori Realities* (2011).

The university today is further overwritten - in the latest in a series of mappings or re-inscriptions - by Auckland's Learning Quarter.[8] The Learning Quarter itself sits within the Auckland council's Supercity-wide vision ('The Auckland Plan') and again promulgates 'liveability', that theme of global currency. Liveability might, of course, be understood in the sense of flourishing rather than financial enrichment or bare fitness for life, although this would require a deeper consideration of the grounds of human deficit about which the term might otherwise make us think. The common ground that is suggested by the local Occupy movement, the We Are The University (WATU) student movement, the University Without Conditions (or free university), and the Tertiary Education Union (TEU), places constitutionality before capitalism. 'Liveable' here refers to well-being, hopefulness and dignity (by contrast, the advent of the 'Pakeha Party' can be read as the expression of a lack of hope, unhinged from history, despairing at the apparent relative advancement of local others, namely Māori). Such developments respond to hurt or injury, and they suggest that real constitutionality - a sense of well-being, hence optimal liveability - are matters of larger environment. Reminding us that the state of global emergency we find ourselves in today is at once military, financial and ecological, they call upon us to reconstruct ground itself, as the recent constitutions of Bolivia and Ecuador do by making the preeminence of Pachamama (earth-being or earth mother) the source for collective flourishing (see Cadena, 2010).

As pressing global and local situations show, the grounds of any claim to universal knowledge are constitutively shaky. In small compass, the physical grounds of the university reveal that local space everywhere is increasingly articulated by lines of fracture, and by interests that are fully implicated in global insecurity (and corresponding surveillance). We do not seek stability amidst such turbulence, but rather embrace the prospect that an overturning of ground, or a returning to ground, might open up a deepened sense of purpose and place. The basis on which we proceed is subtended by questions posed by Te Ahukaramū Charles Royal in terms of Māori knowledge (Mātauranga Māori): 'Who am I? / What is this world that I exist in? What am I to do'? (Royal, 2012) While the Learning Quarter seems to serve as a study in techno-educational enterprise, in geo-theoretical terms it can be re-diagrammed in the form of the buried waters of Horotiu, and in terms of the fault lines that run through it. Such a move both enables and requires us to reconsider the ground of our standing place, which may include prior or other grounds altogether, de-territorialised by settler capitalism. Revisiting sites such as these - attending to our campus itself - calls for

---

[8] See https://cdn.auckland.ac.nz/assets/central/about/the-university/affiliations-associations/documents/learning-quarter.pdf.

reflexive modes of enquiry that do not seek knowledge after or of the fact, but rather re-face public and place in view of disinterred ground, and an unknown commons.

*

... Futures ...

Photograph by Anna Boswell with permission.

In July 2013, the University of Auckland embarked on a large-scale programme of building works centred on its most recently-acquired campus, the site of the former Lion Brewery in the inner suburb of Newmarket. While this 5.2-hectare development seems intended to make a monumentalising statement as the university's own future inheritance (it is, quite literally, the concretisation of strategic planning), microcosmically and metonymically it stands for a set of recurring models. As such, it reveals the predominantly fractal nature of the design-drives to which the university has made itself - or allowed itself to become - subject. Coined in the 1980s by Benoît Mandelbrot, whose work stands as the culmination of centuries of mathematical work on fractional topology, fractality refers to more or less exactly self-similarising patterns which occur at different levels of scale. Mandelbrot noted that coastlines appear equally jagged whether you examine them close up or from further way (Mandelbrot, 1983). Working for IBM, he generated patterns through computer modelling which now dominates work on fractals.

The logic of fractality is strikingly apparent in the rectangularising dream-work of settler-colonialism, which has carved self-similar geopolitical domains (empires, nations, states, regions, conservation lands, agronomic patchwork) into swathes of the globe, and which has supplied precise geometric templates for the gridding of towns and cities. Entirely planned on the surface of the page, such templates are expandable or contractible, enabling them to be adapted for unfolding demographic and economic needs. Such programming tends to be antipathetic to the topological erraticisms of the 'places' that it calls or writes into being, like those encountered and 'corrected' or rectified in the swampy marshlands of what is now Auckland's CBD.

Once you are attuned to it, fractality is readily apparent in the built environments of university campuses, too; universities are, after all, fractal expressions of larger settler-colonial imperatives. The University of Auckland's Owen Glenn business school, for example, reproduces the structure of prominent business school buildings in the US, which in turn reproduce the structures of prominent corporate enterprises (such as IBM); the refurbishment of the Arts 1 building at Auckland reproduces the structure of the Owen Glenn building; and so other university buildings will do the same. Conceived as a 'boom-generator' or hub for STEM subjects (Science, Technology, Engineering, Mathematics) (see Parker, 2010), in fact, the Newmarket campus fractally extends and replicates the Learning Quarter vision of an entrepreneurial eco-system of innovation. The affective dimensions of these fractals are clearly encoded. Space is carved up into self-enclosed cells, regularised according to principles of linearity and angularity, and subject to standardised lighting levels, air flows and temperature controls. Academics are sequestered on the upper levels to get on with their work undisturbed (in order to maximise the research outputs upon which the university's international ranking will be calculated), students are channelled through central reception areas on the ground floor, and teaching rooms are bunkered below.

Fractal modelling is further evident across our city campus in the recently-refurbished offices whose size has been determined through the averaging of office sizes across the G8 universities in Australia (i.e. the top-ranked eight). If, to begin with, no-one in any of these universities actually worked in an office of this size, the proliferation of same-sized offices according to this statistically-determined quantification ensures that Auckland academics and professional staff increasingly do. Such modelling is computationally linked to best practice self-assessment and benchmarking, which work to produce the globally convergent university (the university 2.0). Under these conditions, every university's mission statement, strategic plan and foundational values become the same as every other university's. To be excellent is to be generic, or un-special, in this sense: the atmospherics of excellence are, quite literally, outsourced or plagiarised.

Media coverage of the Newmarket acquisition emphasised the shrewdness of the negotiation and the bargain-basement purchase price.[9] In the public sphere at least, the question of whether the university could afford to 'save' that much has remained virtually un-fielded, while the university's own PR machine has represented the expansion as vital (necessary for life, or life-saving). There can be no question that programmed debts of this kind are meant to secure a university's future livelihood: debt and security are, after all, longtime bedfellows. 'Futures', in this context, seems to refer to stocks, commodities and investments ahead of anything that is palpably human or lived.

The enhanced debt incurred through the Newmarket expansion has already begun to provide pretexts for the further strengthening of management structures, raising of student fees and rationalising of resources (both human and non-human) through cutbacks, redundancies and 'secondments' - which diminish and demonise non-useful, non-STEM subjects.[10] Indeed, the control that is apparent in heightened campus security can be read as the outward manifestation of an acute concern with 'securing' return on investment. The sense of monitoring and surveillance and accountability (or the ability to be called-to-account) that is everywhere evident in campus life is, in other words, a further fractal affect of risk-averse management, as is 'sustainability'. While this much-invoked term always seems to gesture towards something ecological and wholesome, more deeply it means sustainable outlay - that is, debt-ventures that are wholly subject to advance calculations, and that comprehend the health of the whole in terms of an economic pulse.

Such conditions begin to make visible the epistemological and geo-local implications of fractality, and they point towards the fact that as an institution, the university plays a special role in the fractal order. Not only does a university stand as a miniature likeness of society-at-large, but it calls that very society - as idea and practice - into being, producing the large- and small-scale patternings that map out and effect social futures. We may well be troubled, then, by the fact that universities increasingly communicate financial imperatives. As fractal expressions of the larger programme that is the black box of techno-capitalism, they entrench econometric ideas of teaching, learning and knowledge which become manifest at a range of scales. Several recently published genealogies of the modern university have made it clear that education has become ever more

---

[9] See, for example, *New Zealand Herald*, 2013; Ninness, 2012.

[10] These generic processes though which management control has been strengthened at the University of Auckland has been enabled by what is known locally as FAR, the bitterly contested imposition in the last 4 years of the Faculty Administrative Review process.

subject to economic measure since the end of the eighteenth century.[11] While
the foremost drive of education today is ostensibly towards learning that can
be applied (that is, learning with a use-value, or a utility calculus), the deeper
discernible drive is toward learning measurable in econometric terms (that is,
learning with exchange-value, or a market calculus). This commodification of
knowledge makes education a business (*the* business of the university), and it
makes learning calculable in business terms, according to the managerial rhetoric of transparency, efficiency, productivity and so on (a.k.a. Total Quality Management, or TQM).

In practice, econometric imperatives incorporate academics and students
within a larger corporate structure that maps, more or less happily and readily, onto other corporate bodies nationally and transnationally, exemplifying
the preset programming or templating by which techno-capitalism works. The
university's corporatisation makes knowledge a matter of patent and product,
performance and measure, competition and fitness, in order that the institution
itself can become perfectly convergent and fast-following - a drive internalised
by students in view of the 'built pedagogy' of the university environment (Sturm
and Turner, 2011). What we see here is an abdication of the mission to educate, replaced by education as profitable skills and competencies (producing the
portfolio market-making people of the global market that is being expanded).
It turns out that risk and experimentation, where these are not secured by 'sustained' or 'sustaining' examples of self-similar practices elsewhere, are not what
the university means when it claims to foster and value thinking. The risk-averse
'evidence-first' thinking that is actually invoked by this term refers to an infor-
mational model that is, at base, a programme for re-evaluating ideas as data.

Within the fractal academy, then, quantification assumes an ascriptive force,
and the built environment serves merely as the outward manifestation of econometric modelling that is already embedded within management itself. Management ideas, which are necessarily top-down, have an 'elsewhere' quality - that is,
they appear to have always already been applied in other environments. This is
perhaps not strictly as true of real-world environments as it is true of computer
modelling (this is the *wherefrom* or provenance of 'ideas'). Such modelling, or
programming, is the technical substrate of management 'thinking'. If it appears
that *no-one is actually thinking the university*, this is because all decisions are
actually quantities, or pre-quantised data. As this suggests, the 'elsewhereness'
effected by fractality produces a university that can only know itself in and on
terms that are imported from outside, and that will in turn reproduce these
patterns across societal topologies small and large. A university - or a society -
which constructs itself from externally-sourced statistics and dimensions will,
no doubt, picture itself as a space untethered from and accountable to the place
that it occupies, as is the case with international airports and with embassies

---

[11] See, for example, Clark, 2006; Hoskin and Macve, 1986.

situated on foreign soil. Such an entity becomes self-enclosed, vacuum-sealed - an algorithmically generated and genericised 'no-space' where knowledge is groundless because it is alienated from the grounds of its coming-to-be.

*

The Lion Brewery buildings themselves have historically stood for and sustained certain kinds of local knowledges: of the springs that supply the water upon which the brewery was originally founded (and upon which Ngāti Whātua in-habitation of the area was based long before that); of the industrial and commercial footing of the larger settler enterprise; of the compromised nature of the second occupation of this place.[12] Within a few short weeks, however, the Newmarket site has been transformed into a quarry-scape of gutted architectural carcasses and mounds of landfill. Fractally speaking, this ruin represents a new wagon-circle or walled compound, a new locus of emergency. In the face of this rush - to corral, erase, implement, deliver, secure - which is so characteristic of the globally convergent geometries and pedagogies of techno-capitalism and settler-colonialism, it seems timely, to us, to pause. Something is visibly broken here, and though in many ways this is an all-too-common sight, we might learn from the 'uncommon-nesses' of which it is trace.

What the fractal life of programming forecloses is the unstable ground of the university's own operations, to which the university is increasingly closed, but which its own circumscription by measure further and necessarily perturbs. The kind of response that seems called for in this place, then, might be predicated on brokenness and fracture. To imagine fracture as real brokenness - as *dissimilarity* within - is to rupture the very nature of fractal logic: its templating and normativising, its insensitivities to lived difference, its occluding of possibilities for alternate futures and pasts. It is also to think through brokenness itself - to think brokenly - in ways that do not produce symmetries of re-occupation, or mistake part for whole. The grounds of *pre-occupation*, such as those excavated here, offer up means of attunement to self-dissimilar ways of caring for and living well within the place. Such attunement doesn't simply seek to re-face the place, as if it could (in an ongoing sequence of take-overs and make-overs) be remodelled or re-contoured to order. Rather, it re-faces us, requiring us to begin again: uncertain, ungrounded, but here.

References

Cadena, M. de la. 2010. 'Indigenous Cosmopolitics in the Andes; Conceptual Reflections beyond "Politics"'. *Cultural Anthropology* 25.2: 334-370.

---

[12] For a published history of the area see Holman, 2010.

Clark, W. 2006. *Academic Charisma and the Origins of the Research University*. Chicago, IL. University of Chicago Press.

Field, M. 2011. 'Taniwha in the way of Auckland rail loop'. *Stuff.co.nz*. 8 June. Available www.stuff.co.nz/national/5114496/Taniwha-in-the-way-of-Auckland-rail-loop. Accessed 11/11/2013.

Greenway, H.D.S. 2010. 'The Best Place to Live?' *The New York Times*, 26 May. Available http://www.nytimes.com/2010/05/27/opinion/27iht-edgreenway.html.

Accessed 11/11/2013.

Holman, D. 2010. *Newmarket: Lost and Found*. Auckland. The Bush Press.

Hoskin K. and Macve, R. 1986. 'Accounting and the Examination: A Genealogy of Disciplinary Power'. *Accounting, Organisation and Society* 11.2: 105-136.

Jefferson, R.F. 1996. 'Ligar's Canal, Auckland', *Auckland-Waikato Historical Journal* 67: 28-34.

Mandelbrot, B. 1983. *The Fractal Geometry of Nature*. New York, NY. W.H. Freeman.

Mikaere, A. 2002. 'Maori Concepts of Guardianship, Custody and Access: A Literature Review'. August. Ministry of Justice. Available: http://www.justice.govt.nz/publications/publications- archived/2002/guardianship-custody-and-access-maori-perspectives-and-experiences-august-2002/maori-concepts-of-guardianship-custody-and-access-a-literature-review-ani-mikaere-part-two. Accessed 11/11/2013.

_____ . 2011. *Colonising Myths – Māori Realities: He Rukuruku Whakaaro*. Wellington. Huia.

New Zealand Herald. 2013. 'Uni brewery buy endorsed'. 23 April. Available: http://www.nzherald.co.nz/business/news/article.cfm?c_id=3&objectid=10879168. Accessed 19/06/2015.

Ninness, G. 2012. 'Huge wins and losses in Lion deal'. 23 September. Available: http://www.stuff.co.nz/auckland/local-news/7717110/Huge-wins-and-losses-in-Lion-deal. Accessed 19/06/2015.

Parker, M. 2010. *The Pine Tree Paradox: Why Creating the New Zealand We All Dream of Requires a Great University*. New Plymouth. PublishMe.

Radio New Zealand News. 2011. 'Taniwha no threat to tunnel project, iwi says'. 9 June. Available: http://www.radionz.co.nz/news/national/77301/taniwha-no-threat-to-tunnel-project,-iwi-says. Accessed 19/06/2015.

Rancière, J. 2006. *The Politics of Aesthetics: The Distribution of the Sensible*. London. Continuum.

Round, D. 2011. 'Horotiu the taniwha stirs'. 2 July. Available: http://www.nzcpr.com/horotiu-the-taniwha-stirs/. Accessed 05/11/2013.

Royal, T.E.C. 2012. 'Politics and Knowledge: Kaupapa Māori and mātauranga Māori'. *New Zealand Journal of Educational Studies / Te Hautaki Mātai o Aotearoa* 45.2: 30-37.

Sturm, S., and Turner, S. 2011. '"Built pedagogy": The University of Auckland Business School as Crystal Palace'. *Interstices: A Journal of Architecture and Related Arts* 12: 23-34.

Twyford, P. 2011. 'Who is the real taniwha here?' *Red Alert*. 9 June. Available: http://blog.labour.org.nz/2011/06/09/who-is-the-real-taniwha-here/. Accessed 11/11/2011.

VISITING HOURS:
GUIDED TOURS OF THE CARCERAL THEMEPARK

Sophie Fuggle

Welcome to Deadman Wonderland

In a not so distant dystopic future, Tokyo is 70% underwater following severe earthquakes. The city is being rebuilt but funding is lacking. Welcome to *Deadman Wonderland* (Kadokawa, 2013), a prison turned theme park where inmates compete in order to stay alive in front of tourists come for a fun family day out. The death is real but the spectacle is fake. Visitors believe it's simply a show put on for their benefit with death an optical illusion simulated by a load of high quality special effects. Profits generated go to the reconstruction of the city.

The only survivor of a high school massacre, Nagano, has been framed for the murder of his classmates. Incarcerated at Deadman Wonderland, he must compete in various competitions in order to buy the antidote to the slow-acting poison given to all inmates. His success and survival must invariably, if indirectly, come at the cost of that of the other prisoners against whom he his pitted. This is a well-known formula found not only in manga series like *Deadman Wonderland* but perhaps better recognized in films such as *The Running Man* (1987) and *Battle Royale* (2000) along with novels such as DBC Pierre's *Vernon God Little* (2003) and the primetime TV series *Prison Break* (2005-9). The protagonist as homo sacer (Agamben, 1998) within the space of the prison turned game show, the amusement park cum assault course.

As viewer or reader, we form a second layer audience to the fictional spectators come to see criminals perform and compete for their lives. Privy to the backstory of the characters who are forced to run the gauntlet or, in the case of *Vernon God Little*, have their fate decided by telephone vote, we, this second audience, root for the innocent protagonist, whose crime is either absent or doesn't fit the extremity of the punishment being meted out. At the same time, we assume a position of smug superiority and disgust towards the fictional audiences who revel in the spectacle of torture and death. Yet, our complicity should also be noted. Little reflection is spared upon those 'real' criminals our heroes come up against. Who cares what happens in the Thunderdome as long as Mad Max gets out alive? Does it matter how many murderers and rapists die not to mention unscrupulous politicians and thuggish correctional officers as part of Michael Schofield's struggle to save his brother, Lincoln, from the death penalty in *Prison Break*? Frequently, these supporting characters, depicted as pure brawn, expendable flesh or pantomime villains[1] with nothing between the two poles of caricature, provide a legitimation in terms of plot function of the very modes of punishment required by a society in which all the characters are trying to eke out an existence. Is this not also the way those in today's penal system are more often than not presented to us? Monsters like Ian Brady or mindless, unskilled, uneducated, faceless youths, disposable labour to be warehoused in the most efficient means possible until the economy so requires? The implicit morality at stake in such fictional and non-fictional representation lies in the corruption or failure of a system via certain individuals not the system of punishment itself. So it seems.

*

The reason I open with a reference to a Japanese manga cartoon is because it alerts us to various questions concerning the space of the prison within contemporary society. I want to suggest that the concept of prison turned game show or even theme park does not belong only in some distant dystopia. Rather, it is useful for thinking through the way in which we engage with the space of the prison today, the way it forms part of our infrastructure and the way in which it simultaneously is set aside, set up, fenced off as an exceptional space yet at the same time inextricably bound up in the rhythms of everyday existence in the same way that a theme park is.

Moreover, to what extent is the prison already framed as theme park? I do not only mean family outings to Alcatraz or the Tower of London here, the type of sites referred to by Michael Welch as an inverted Disneyland (Welch, 2015) but also the guided tour of the working prison, the narratives of prison life curated by museums and art galleries, the documentaries which, much like the video console, bring the exhilaration of the prison as theme park into the space of the home, conveniently and safely framed within the space of the screen. Where the latter, the prison documentary, constitutes, alongside fictional representations of prison life, a problematic rendering of the prison as theme park, game show or carnivalesque space, during this chapter, I would like to focus my discussion on the actual rather than virtual engagement of the 'docile' body as it navigates the space of the prison as pedagogical exercise, regulated encounter with the dangerous 'other', work of art or historical artifact.

It is also worth noting here that my discussion concentrates on the prison as the site housing those who, to all intents and purposes, have been tried and

---

[1] More sustained, insightful comments on pantomime villains in Hutnyk (2014).

sentenced according to the requirements of a functioning justice system. The prison perceived as exceptional space but an institutional space nonetheless. A space which confines those society generally agrees *deserve* to be there as a result of breaking established laws before being proved by a civilian jury to have done so. I am not talking about the 'camp' here. I am not talking about Guantanamo or Abu Ghraib or the military prison where Chelsea Manning is serving out her sentence. These are sites in which space and time are suspended along with justice and human rights. The discourses and debates contesting their existence are frequently underpinned by the assumption that other, 'regular' carceral spaces are, and indeed should be, taken for granted. Moreover, it is precisely as a result of being predicated upon different logics (the exceptional vs. the everyday) that the war industry and the prison industry are able to legitimate one another so effectively.

Following some more general reflections on how the ideology, structure and operation of the theme park might be mapped onto the prison, my analysis is based on a series of observations made during a tour of Attica in 2012. As an academic 'tourist' from a large metropolis, the most striking of these was the extent to which the prison continues to function according to a disciplinary logic rather than a more deterritorialised form of power associated with a globalized, digitized twenty-first century. In this respect, the prison draws our attention to the ongoing role of Fordism within society not as a residue but operating alongside newer forms of social control and management of the labour force. Pursuing the notion of 'theme park' further, I will then consider the emergence of the heritage site as contemporary reimagining of the peripheral leisure space and the ways in which the space of the prison also operates according to similar processes of 'museification'. Throughout my readings are indebted both to Theodor Adorno's critique of what he and Max Horkheimer termed the 'culture industry' and Michel Foucault's notion of disciplinary power developed in *Discipline and Punish* (1977).

Open to the Public

When it opened in 1955, Disneyland marked a shift in the spatial configuration of entertainment and leisure in relation to work and to a certain extent set in motion the processes by which outdoor, public space was increasingly regulated and privatized. Located off the highway at a significant distance from Los Angeles and any public transport links, access to Disneyland was limited to those in possession of a car thus defining itself in relation to a certain emerging social class. Where each ride was ticketed, there was an additional entrance fee to the park itself marking it out as a different experience and economic investment to temporary fairgrounds and the public parks of city centres.

In its clear demarcation of free time within a fenced-off space, on the margins, rather than at the centre of the urban sprawl, the theme park enforced the bracketing out of free time from that of work in concrete form. Yet, at the same time, the organization, management and regulation of the theme park with its entrance fees, queues and scheduled appearances from Mickey and Minnie, replicated the disciplinary apparatus found in the factory and office. Free time, as Adorno put it, is not simply defined as such in contradistinction to the rest of the time, i.e., work time, but is also 'shackled to its opposite', dependent upon 'the totality of social conditions which continues to hold people under its spell' (Adorno, 1991).

At the same time as it forcibly separated the work and leisure spaces of the upwardly mobile masses, the theme park required its own labour force and an entire industrial complex developed in and around its confines. It is these inherent spatial contradictions in which the theme park functions simultaneously as peripheral space and central hub around which entire towns and communities are based that also define that which Angela Davis (2003) refers to as the 'prison industrial complex.' Like the theme park, the prison operates as a contained space on the margins of society, its role is also to absorb the excesses, the surpluses of economic production. Where in the theme park these excesses consist of the disposable income, physical energy and boredom of the compliant worker, in the space of the prison, it is the surplus labour that is quarantined.

In Post-Fordist, late capitalist society, the delineations between workplace and leisure space become increasingly blurred. Work has now been reimagined as a form of 'play', playtime now openly acknowledged as the continuation of the working day. Emotional labour and reward now complicate and confuse the straightforward relationship between work and salary. The city has morphed into a giant theme park defined by Michael Sorkin as follows:

> This is the meaning of the theme park, the place that embodies it all, the ageographia, the surveillance and control, the simulations without end. The theme park presents its happy regulated vision of pleasure – all those artfully hoodwinking forms – as a substitute for the democratic public realm, and it does so appealingly by stripping troubled urbanity of its sting, of the presence of the poor, of crime, of dirt, of work. (Sorkin, 1992)

Sorkin identifies three key characteristics defining the contemporary city – the ruptures with local and cultural geography produced by globalized, digitized flows of capital, information and identity, the increased segregation produced by pervasive surveillance technologies and, finally, the endless proliferation of simulations and semiotics within the cityscape. If Sorkin's lamentations, written over twenty years ago, have become all too obvious to appear worth reiterating, I want to suggest we push against this reading of city as theme park in order to resist the apathetic resignation to the alienation inherent in such a reading.

According to such a reading, the prison cell ceases to represent a fixed space located on the distant horizon of the bloated urban landscape and has now crept into the city itself, deterritorialised as an abstract, psychological concept or wireless, digital application in the form of electronic tracking devices. To some extent, we are all in shackles, all under observation. Yet, it is clear that the everyday experience of the average service industry worker, professional or executive is not comparable with that of those carrying out a prison sentence in a penal institution. Being expected to respond to e-mails on your Blackberry during a family meal is not of the same order as having to shit in a room shared with two other people. More attention to the specific material realities of physical space is needed as a counterpoint to much contemporary urban theory which, in identifying the homogenizing effects of recent urban planning and development, risks repeating the same gesture, reducing all space to homogeneous zones of alienation, surveillance and mindless consumption.

With this in mind, I want to return to the original conceptions of theme park and prison as exterior containers of the surpluses of economic production. Where free time and entertainment have become increasingly integrated into a working life no longer bound by the factory gates, clock-in cards or timesheets, the prison continues to function according to the spatio-temporal parameters defined by its physical location and architecture.[2] Moreover, in its persistence on the horizon as exceptional space, the prison has come to assume the role once played by the theme park. Where the theme park was designed according to the dual demands of nostalgia and novelty which in the case of Disneyland took the form of different historical (Frontierland) and futuristic (Tomorrowland) sectors juxtaposed with one another, the dialectic also plays out within the space of the prison. If the aim of the prison documentary is to present us with the 'novel' perspective of life on the inside, the prison tour, elaborated upon in the following section, is taken up with the historical contextualization of current day practices and operation.

Planning your visit

What is the purpose of a prison tour? Who is granted access? Who gets invited to see what goes on within the walls, behind the bars? With the advent of widely distributed documentary series such as MSNBC's *Lockup* franchise, there is the sense that we are all invited. Invited to participate in a certain narrative of incarceration in which those locked up are incited to define themselves according to a series of stereotypes – recidivist, pervert, boss, soldier, bitch, snitch and so on. First time offenders arrive in prison with a preconceived notion of prison life and how they should 'perform' their role here. Yet, where the prison filtered

---

[2] For further analysis of the carceral 'time-space', see Moran (2012).

through our television screens is, predominantly aimed at legitimizing the penal system via the setting up, and occasional critique, of such stereotypes, the prison tour functions altogether differently. Rather than presenting the outside world with the full force of the menace posed by those incarcerated, what visitors are shown (assuming all goes to plan) is the neutralization of the criminal 'threat', legitimizing the space of the prison via the various mechanisms of discipline and control structuring its operation. These two modes – the exaggerated menace and the perfectly oiled prison machine – work together, not only removing all abolitionist discourse from the debate but simultaneously suppressing or severely limiting any sustained argument for prison reform.

Where in the U.S. tour buses arriving at the gates of prisons like Attica include a range of different 'publics' including high school children,[3] nosy academics and filmmakers, elsewhere such as in France, access is more carefully regulated and still tends to be limited to politicians, senior level officials and, when deemed necessary, hand-picked journalists.[4] The work of the *Groupe d'information sur les prisons* [Prisons Information Group or GIP] during the early 1970s in France, sought to highlight and redress the way access to prisons was so heavily regulated along with the details of their conditions and organization. The information gathered by the group thanks to the help of former detainees, families, lawyers, social workers, doctors – all those involved with the working of the prison but in some way at odds with its logic and operation – was presented in a series of pamphlets entitled 'Enquête sur l'intolérable.' Alongside prisoners' responses to questions about the material and psychological conditions of prison life, the group provided critique, commentary and reflection on the state and ideology of penal systems in France and beyond. Where members of the group were precluded from entering prisons themselves in order to speak to prisoners and employees, they nevertheless provided an excellent commentary on the specific nature and function of the prison 'tour'.

As Alain Brossat has pointed out, media interest in France's prisons usually occurs after a high profile scandal that the prison authorities were unable to contain or diffuse. Journalists flock to the site, a few outraged reports are published on the dismal condition of the prison system, interviews with key prison

---

[3] We should also acknowledge the amalgamation of these two modes of presenting the prison in the form of documentary series like *Scared Straight* in which unruly high school kids spend time in a penitentiary as a deterrent against further bad behaviour.

[4] The varying attitude towards public tours of carceral spaces no doubt has much to do with the management and financing of the penal system. Where in the U.S. the prison, penitentiary or supermax constitutes an industrial complex, outsourced to private contractors, elsewhere, the penal system remains a state-run institution. Whether the prison is considered first and foremost in terms of the income it generates, the 'social' role it plays in educating and 'rehabilitating' offenders, or the total exclusion of the 'criminal' body from society it enacts - the complicity or non-complicity in public perceptions and fictional and non-fictional representations of prison life are culturally inflected according to these different ideologies.

employees are conducted then heavily edited into sound bites then all is forgotten until the next scandal. Within this cycle of moral indignation and indifference, the guided prison tour functions to alleviate whilst giving the appearance of openly inviting criticism by carefully selecting the right (leaning) reporters and conducting them around a meticulously planned circuit of a well-chosen prison (Brossat, 2002).

Built in the 1960s as a 'model' prison and currently still the largest prison in Europe, Fleury-Mérogis was the subject of a rare report on prisons by the mainstream newspaper *France Soir* in March 1971. Having been taken on a tour of the prison, journalist Jean Feriot reported that

> N'était la présence de gardiens qui portent au revers de leur vareuse l'étoile dorée de leur administration, n'était l'existence de grilles qu'ont dirait conçues par un spécialiste du « design », Fleury-Mérogis pourrait passer – que les gauchistes n'en tirent pas argument – pour une université, longs couloirs clairs, salles spacieuses, larges terrains de jeux. (Feriot, 1971 ctd in Groupe d'Information sur les prisons, 1971)

> [If it wasn't for the presence of the guards bearing the gold star of the prison administration on their uniform, or the existence of bars said to be conceived by a design expert, Fleury-Mérogis might be mistaken – which the lefties will no doubt try to use for their own ends – for a university with long, bright corridors, spacious rooms and large sports pitches.] (my translation)

After gushing over all the different activities available to the inmates, Feriot concludes his article as follows :

> Peut-être certains de mes lecteurs vont-ils ricaner, hausser les épaules ou s'indigner, dire que « ces voyous ne méritent pas de tels égards» ou que « tout ca c'est du cinéma ». Ma réaction, à moi, est différente. Si je regrette que toutes les prisons de France ne ressemblent pas à Fleury-Mérogis, je déplore surtout que de tels efforts soient déployés par la société pour rendre à des adolescents la dignité que cette même société s'est employée à leur faire perdre.

> [Perhaps some of my readers will scoff, shrug their shoulders or get indignant, saying that 'these yobs don't deserve such consideration' or that 'it's all a show'. My personal reaction is different. While I lament the fact that not all prisons in France resemble Fleury-Mérogis, I find it particularly deplorable that society does not go to the same lengths to give adolescents back the dignity, it took away from them.] (my translation)

Reproducing, Feriot's article in a pamphlets dedicated to Fleury-Mérogis, the GIP prefaced this with a commentary on the function and orchestration of the prison tour aimed at producing precisely the type of narrative provided by Feriot:

> On fait passer très vite les visiteurs dociles, on les laisse s'arrêter aux endroits prévus, interroger ici ou là des surveillants qui font bonne figure et qui savent,

convaincus ou non, tenir des propos rassurants sur la rareté des punitions et sur la réinsertion sociale du détenu. On montre ensuite un atelier un peu actif, une activité sportive un peu vivante.

On laisse ensuite au visiteur content le soin de généraliser dans sa tête, de penser que ce qu'il a vu, c'est ce qui se passe tous les jours et dans toute la prison.'

[The docile visitors are shown around quickly, stopping only in pre-arranged locations where now and again they have the chance to interview those guards who present themselves best and, whether convinced or not, know how to proffer up reassuring accounts concerning the rarity of punishments and the rehabilitation of prisoners. Then the visitors are shown a lively (but not too lively) workshop and some energetic (but not too energetic) sports activity.

The satisfied visitor is then left to form his own generalizations, to draw the conclusion that what he has seen corresponds to what happens everyday throughout the entire prison.] (my translation)

The irony, however, the commentary goes on to conclude is that Feriot plays his role a little too well, offering a eulogy of the prison that in its misty-eyed romanticism embarrasses rather than satisfies those who set it up. To enthuse too much about the prison tour risks exposing the fragile myth of rehabilitation that Feriot is desperate to subscribe to. Like the theme park, the prison tour cannot but fail to disappoint. Either it is so well-managed it appears as the hollow, staged event that it is. Not well-organised enough and the anxieties it was intended to alleviate return all the more forcibly. In seeking to compensate for his disappointment, Feriot's rhetoric reproduces the parody.

Postcard from Attica

Where the work of the GIP emerged as a response to the heavily regulated access to prisons in France, it was, inevitably, also impeded by these restrictions. Members of the group were unable to visit prisoners, who were only allowed to see lawyers and close family members, or to see how the inside of a prison operated on a day-to-day basis. In the 1950s Foucault had spent time working as Jacqueline Verdeaux's assistant at the 'Centre National d'Orientation' at Fresnes Prison. This 'unofficial' access had put him in contact with a wide range of different inmates and was no doubt of major importance in shaping his understanding of the relationship between criminology and psychiatry (Macey, 1993). Yet, during his involvement with the GIP, Foucault did not enter a prison until after the work of the group had mostly ceased, giving way to prisoner-led activist groups such as the Comité d'Action des Prisonniers (CAP) and the Association pour la Défense des Droits des Détenus (ADDD). And this visit, twenty years after

Fresnes, was not in France but in the U.S. In January 1972, Foucault visited Attica prison in upstate New York. The previous year, it had seen the worst riots in U.S. penal history with inmates taking over the prison for 4 days before state troopers stormed the prison, killing 39 people including 10 guards and civilians employed at the prison. In a short piece written on Attica, Foucault describes his impressions of the prison as follows:

> At Attica what struck me perhaps first of all was the entrance, that kind of phony fortress à la Disneyland, those observation posts disguised as medieval towers with their machicoulis. And behind this rather ridiculous scenery which dwarfs everything else, you discover that it's an immense machine… (translated and cited in Macey, 1993)

The GIP's critique of prisons as the most 'intolerable' of all public institutions[5] seems to be predicated on a more Althusserian notion of Ideological State Apparatuses (Althusser, 1971) than on the complex power/knowledge relations articulated by Foucault in *Discipline and Punish* and beyond. At the same time the GIP project entertains the idea that giving prisoners the chance to speak for themselves could conceivably lead to a more engaged public critique of both ideology and operation of prisons. That such testimonies might ultimately be appropriated by the prison and its mechanisms, resulting in more efficient management of the self-defined rather than interpellated criminal body seems largely absent from the GIP's statements and analyses. Moreover, where the prison riots that occurred in Nancy and other French prisons were taken up by the GIP as moments of freedom, defined by assertions of agency on the part of the prisoners, visiting Attica in the aftermath of the riots produced an altogether different response from Foucault to the understanding of power he presented in his 1971 lectures. Here, power is presented as essentially repressive. Foucault's expectation prior to visiting Attica was that the prison was an essentially exclusionary apparatus rather than a more complex disciplinary machine aimed at both producing the criminal subject as such and, at the same time, rendering this subject into a 'docile' body.

*

Visiting Attica in March 2012, it soon became clear the extent to which the prison continues to operate in the shadow of the riots. The whole system at Attica is intended to produce docile bodies. During the tour, which lasted about two hours, we passed numerous prisoners in the hallway who not only didn't speak but also didn't make any form of eye contact since they can get 'written up' for this. Being written up is part of a complicated system of rewards and

---

[5] Statement on the back cover of the *Intolérable* pamphlets. Reproduced in Artières (2013).

deprivations. There were a series of yellow lines marked in the hallways but also in communal areas like the workshop - prisoners would stop and wait behind these until instructed to do otherwise as if obeying a complex traffic system. In this sense, the prison infrastructure seems to embody the type of circulation only dreamed of by city planners. It is a system which defines itself not in terms of the speed and fluidity with which individuals can move through it but, rather, in the control of movement and the patient acceptance of those moving (and stopping) within it.

'There are no demonstrations in Disneyland' (Sorkin, 1992). No riots either. Similarly, the self-interest and focus on instant gratification which Sorkin suggests defines the theme park, perhaps reaches its apotheosis within the space of present day Attica. Today, if a prisoner kicks off it is usually a response to some immediate deprivation like no ketchup. A C.O. (correctional officer) lamented the days when prisoners would think more strategically, even organise their resistance. In the 1980s, prisoners would freak out the guards by eating in silence in the mess hall. 400 inmates all complicit in the same passive act of defiance. Now, there is no organisation, no solidarity, no long-term strategy either for resistance or improved conditions. The C.O. both blamed and thanked crack for this. His job is easier but he seems to respect the prisoners (and perhaps as a consequence his role in managing them) less.

That the correctional officers and all those working in the prison are subject to the same disciplinary mechanisms organizing the prison as those detained there is perhaps obvious. Nevertheless, the extent to which the prison continues to operate according to a Fordist factory model is striking. When asked what the most rewarding aspect of his job was, the C.O. told us, with no irony, that it was 'getting to leave at 3 every afternoon'. On being pushed further, he conceded that better still was his impending retirement on a full pension. Where most of the Western world has long abandoned the 40-40-40 model (or in the U.S. a 50-50-50 model), with most people having no real idea about how many hours are actually worked each week, each year or how to fund their retirement, here in the space of Attica, multiple generations of C.O.s have done the same time before being let out for the same good behaviour. In a blue-collar town such as Attica, there is still honour in choosing the same profession as your father and his father before. Besides, there are few other options. The guards like the prisoners are caught up in the disciplinary space of the prison. Everyone has a place and everyone knows where it is.

On arriving at Attica at 8am in the morning, the first thing that is striking is the number of cars parked outside. Visiting hours were not yet under way and the visitors parking area is relatively small compared to the huge number of SUVs and other vehicles, all of which belong to staff working in the prison. There are 2,200 prisoners, 500 guards and about 300 other members of staff.

However, we were told by the C.O. that the prisoners do much of the work needed in the prison themselves. Without wishing to reproduce the hyperbole of Feriot's account, the prison was spotless, prisoners do all the gardening and cooking. There is a metal workshop which produces large metal cabinets mostly for use, I gather, in industrial and public institutions like hospitals and schools. The C.O. told us that due to union labour laws, many organisations refuse or are not allowed to buy items produced in prisons (inmates get paid approximately 60 cents a day to be in prison). To get round these laws, parts are sent out to be assembled elsewhere then sold. The C.O. was unapologetic about this to the point of indignation. From his perspective, the prison needs to be financially viable and has been hit by the recession along with all manufacturing in the U.S.

Here, the dogged work ethic of the Fordist factory worker rubs up against both older and newer versions of the relationship between industry, labour and criminality. First and foremost, prison labour constitutes one of the legacies of slavery (Davis, 2003). As Angela Davis points out, not only did punishments previously associated with slavery become integrated into the penal system but the system itself became preoccupied with the organisation and control of 'black labour' via the convict lease and county chain gang.

Yet, at the same time, the presentation of such 'labour' as a privilege, offered only to an elite few within the prison, seems more akin to the 'emotional' investment in labour which belongs to a post-Fordist, neoliberal work environment. This is the precarious labour of the creative and culture industries, the zero hours contracts of freelance designers, performers and educators, a rite of passage for the arrogant and greedy, the graduate interns demonstrating their prowess by pulling all-nighters at Goldman Sachs with minimal chance of a contract at the end of their soul destroying, red-bull fuelled stint. But where the young, over-educated and naively ambitious can still cling desperately to the myth of success, there is no such myth here in Attica. There is no discourse of rehabilitation. And with manufacturing rapidly declining in the U.S., it is unlikely the skills acquired within the workshop will enhance the possibilities of employment on the outside. Which left me wondering as to the end, if not slavery, of this unpaid labour?

All programmes in the prison whether education or work-based are seen as a means of keeping prisoners busy and situated in the complex system of privileges that can be taken away for any form of bad behaviour. The dismissal of any lasting value to the programmes offered in the prison by the C.O. also attests to a certain ideology running throughout U.S. society. Prisoners cannot be seen to be benefiting from their time in prison or using it to give themselves any sort of competitive advantage. The tax-paying public resent the idea of any form of assistance which might actually help people improve their situation because that would, in turn, threaten the privileged position of those 'providing' the assistance. So, while many universities offer degree programmes to prisoners, these are not something the universities are always keen to promote or even mention. The fear is that the wealthy parents of their regular students will object to paying for the children to obtain the same piece of paper as someone in prison - who gets it for free. Prison is a warehouse, keeping the surpluses of the labour force on ice until required by the economy. This is why prison is often considered as a revolving door. This is also why Bill Clinton introduced the 3-strikes law in 1994.

Moreover, to what extent does this process of warehousing begin long before the prison? In schools, detention centres, foster homes? Davis suggests that 'when children attend schools that place a greater value on discipline and security than on knowledge and intellectual development, they are attending prep schools for prison' (Davis, 2003). The management of excess bodies whose labour is surplus and whose presence acts as a threat does not just occur within the interior of the exterior space of the penitentiary. Here, Attica simply operates as the end point. There is nowhere else to go. And perhaps there never was. Its statistics, racial demographics, rates of recidivism, drug use and AIDS infection affirm rather than condemn the process.

Exhibit A.

Where the World Fairs of the early twentieth century along with the theme and amusement parks that came later all focused on the 'universal' – the condensation of multiple 'worlds' and 'lands' into a couple of hectares - in recent years there has been a shift in focus to the 'local' and 'particular'. The heritage site with its claims to educate and preserve a specific historical building or town is redefining the notion of the theme park, offering a long overdue riposte to Adorno's scathing indictment of the culture industry. Such pretensions are no less sinister in their calculating appropriation of the masses in the service of their cause than amusement parks and prime time television ever were. The pseudo-artisanal cola served in the cafes and restaurants at places of historical interest tastes no better, and usually worse, than Coca-Cola yet costs twice as much. All this really amounts to is what Giorgio Agamben calls the 'museification' of the world (Agamben, 2007). Free time is no longer spent on physical activities but on artifacts, things in glass cabinets and frames. Objects and experiences bracketed out from the world, frozen in time, removed from any 'use value.' To fill one's free time with the perfectly preserved, neatly framed object lends legitimacy to one's labour time. Work-time is also frozen time.

As mentioned earlier, the prison operates according to the very logic of nostalgia and novelty that embodies this paralyzing process of museification. Attica is in many senses a museum, a long-running exhibition on the riots of 1971. Beyond the memorial statue outside the prison, a more literal example can be found on the wall outside the family visiting room. Here, there is a mounted glass cabinet filled with weapons and tattoo needles, which have, over the years, been confiscated by prisoners. It is unclear whether these serve as a warning to potential smugglers, a celebration of vigilance on the part of the guards or a grudging respect to the ingenuity of the inmates. Possibly all three.

Equally ambiguous in its display choices was an exhibition, *Separation and Silence*, charting the history of Wandsworth prison to the present day which ran at Wandsworth Museum in South London during 2011.[6] Where the exhibition began with artifacts such as truncheons carved by inmates for use by the guards, accounts on the severe restrictions on communication between prisoners including veils worn by those in the women's wing, it swiftly progressed to a display of various patchwork quilts sewn by prisoners and put on show the previous year at the Victoria and Albert Museum in Central London. The quilts were accompanied by video clips of the inmates talking about the life-changing experience of learning to sew and make the quilts.

The rhetoric of rehabilitation assumed by the inmates was clearly intended to be viewed by visitors as a welcome contrast to the earlier days of physical oppression and the limitations placed on the free speech of prisoners. The ambiguity lies in the extent to which we are expected to take such rhetoric seriously and to what end? The appropriation of this discourse of rehabilitation seems to lend itself to the same parody as Feriot's over-enthusiastic declarations following his visit to Fleury-Mérogis. Where all discussion of rehabilitation seemed moot in Attica despite the range of programmes and activities on offer, here, the potential of embroidery appears overstated to the point of ridicule. What the two positions have in common is an appreciation of the criminal, incarcerated body as possessing an inherent economic value. In the case of the U.S. system, such a value is indexed to labour power in the form of blue-collar factory work and where this fails it is either warehoused, kept in a docile state of suspension or given over to the spectacle of the prison documentary. In the U.K. it is the criminal body's potential for self-representation, reproducing itself in and as a work of art that constitutes its economic value and cultural currency. Criminal as artwork as commodity.

In recent years, literature and artwork produced by inmates in various U.K. prisons has constituted the focus of a series of high profile exhibitions headed up by the Koestler Trust's *Art by Offenders*. The Southbank hosts an annual exhibition of this work in its 'Spirit Level' space, based around themes such as 'Catching Dreams' (2014) and 'The Strength and Vulnerability Bunker' (2013).

---

[6] Having made reference to both French and U.S. penal systems, consideration of this 'gallery' phenomenon working its way across U.K. prisons adds a further cultural inflection. To attend to such inflections is not to express a preference for one particular discourse of incarceration above another thus risking acquiescence with the *logic* of incarceration *per se* but, rather, to consider how each functions to legitimize the penal system within a certain socio-economic framework.

Here the culture industry meets the prison industry head on. Sustained reflection or criticism of the public policy and ideological agendas underpinning such initiatives seems to have been circumvented by the unquestioning, ubiquitous approval and the routine trotting out of clichés concerning the emancipatory role of art for all who encounter it. A series of objects crafted in prison are put on display in these exhibitions, offering up a heady blend of exoticism and comfort as the criminal body is rendered docile, productive body within the contours of the objects. The real, ethico-moral, physical and material conditions of possibility of such objects lend them a certain authenticity, an aura. An aura that is not simply decaying, as Adorno suggested, but writhing around in violent agony, forced to eat its own intestines while we watch and nod in contemplative approval.

Conclusion: Escape Through the Gift Shop

To see inside a prison whether on an official visit, via media images or through the textual and artistic self-representations of inmates is not to 'see' a prison but precisely to avoid seeing. Echoing Roland Barthes' critique of 'shock photography' (Barthes, 1957) - the graphic images of contemporary prison documentaries (particularly those coming from the U.S.) which claim to show the viewer everything function in the same way as Jean Feriot's article – both reassure the reader and viewer that they need not really see, both assume the legitimacy of the space of the prison, its organization and functioning. Likewise, art and writing produced during incarceration is rabidly consumed as a form of liberal philanthropy by affluent, left wing intellectuals. The frisson of subversion combined with smug charity absorbs any genuine debate on the penal system and the subjectivities it engenders.

The commodification of criminality in the U.S. via prison labour, private management contracts and the political economy of warehousing whole chunks of the population rather than providing the adequate education, healthcare and welfare support on the outside is well-documented as is the export of the model of the prison industrial complex to Europe and beyond. In addition to the symbiotic relationship between war on terror and war on drugs, discourses of national and local security there is also an emerging alignment between the culture and prison industries. Drawing on public obsession for the authentic encounter with the transgressive other, the prison becomes theme park, game show and art installation.

Little stretch of the imagination is required to envisage a moment in which the slinging of shit by those spending 23 hours a day in solitary confinement in the supermaxes as a last ditch attempt at free expression is offered as pay-per-view entertainment, the soiled walls and bars then auctioned off to private art collectors.

References

Adorno, T. 1991. *The Culture Industry: Selected Essays on Mass Culture*. London and New York, NY. Routledge.

Agamben, G. 1998. *Homo Sacer: Sovereign Power and Bare Life*. Stanford, CA. Stanford University Press.

_____ . 2007. *Profanations*. New York, NY. Zone Books.

Althusser, L. 'Ideology and Ideological State Apparatuses' in *Lenin and Philosophy and Other Essays*. London. New Left Books. 127-88.

Barthes, R. 1957. *Mythologies*. Paris. Seuil.

Brossat, A. 2002. *Pour en finir avec la prison*. Paris. Editions la fabrique.

Davis, A.Y. 2003. *Are Prisons Obsolete?* New York, NY. Seven Stories Press.

Feriot, J. 1971. 'Une prison différente' *France Soir*. 13 March.

Foucault, M. 1977. *Discipline and Punish*. Translated by Alan Sheridan. London. Penguin.

Groupe d'Information sur les prisons. 1971. *Intolérable 2*. Paris. Champ Libre.

Hutnyk, J. 2014. *Pantomime Terror*. London: Zero Books.

Kadokawa, J. 2013. *Deadman Wonderland Volume 1*. San Francisco, CA. Viz Media.

Macey, D. 1993. *The Lives of Michel Foucault*. London. Hutchinson.

Moran, D. 2012. '"Doing Time in Carceral Space": Timespace and Carceral Geography'. *Geografiska Annaler: Series B, Human Geography* 94.4: 305–316.

Pierre, D.B.C. 2003. *Vernon God Little*. London. Faber & Faber.

Sorkin, M. (ed.) 1992. *Variations on a Theme Park: The New American City and the End of Public Space*. New York, NY. Noonday Press.

Welch, M. 2015. *Escape to Prison: Penal Tourism and the Pull of Punishment*. Oakland, CA. University of California Press.

www.ingramcontent.com/pod-product-compliance
Lightning Source LLC
Chambersburg PA
CBHW051439270326
41931CB00020B/3481